ALSO BY ELEANOR CLARK

The Bitter Box

Rome and a Villa

The Oysters of Locmariaquer

Baldur's Gate

Dr. Heart: A Novella and Other Stories

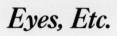

Eyes, Etc.

Eyes, Etc.

A Memoir

BY

ELEANOR CLARK

Pantheon Books, New York

Library of Congress Cataloging in Publication Data
Clark, Eleanor, 1913-
Eyes, Etc.
1. Clark, Eleanor, 1913- —Biography.
2. Authors, American—20th century—Biography.
I. Title.
PS3505.L254Z52   813'.5'4 [B]   77-76505
ISBN 0-394-41550-7

Sections of this book, in somewhat different form, have
appeared in the following magazines: *The Atlantic
Monthly, Commentary, The Georgia Review, The Southern
Review, Vogue,* and *The Yale Review.*

Manufactured in the United States of America

FIRST EDITION

To Sylvia Marlowe

... though my Soul more bent
To serve therewith my Maker, and present
My true account ...

—JOHN MILTON

Preface

If the writer of what follows could at the time have named the affliction, written the nasty words, there'd be no such pages. Not glaucoma anyway, nothing she'd ever heard of before though not too uncommon, they say. One eye first, three years earlier; that's all right, rotten for tennis but not bad otherwise. Then the second. Massive retinal hemorrhages beyond laser treatment, leaving permanent scar tissue and known by the bleary name of macular degeneration. Loss of sight far from total. Job must have looked pretty lucky too to some of the neighbors.

Time and place: first Vermont, summer of 1976, starting a few months after the—well, the event, to call it something; ending that fall in Connecticut. The chronicle, to call *it* something, didn't start as a book. It was written on huge drawing pads, in Magic Markers, of which it took about a hundred before it was over. They're great but don't hold up very long under real trouble.

Not coincidentally, during the period of the writing, evenings were spent in readings—aloud, of course—of the Iliad and the Odyssey, and they are inseparable from the rest of the story. No erudition about Homer claimed or aimed for; couldn't have been; the epics are dealt with simply as the crucial part of life they were for those months and will remain.

The translation used was Robert Fitzgerald's and a splendid one it is for reading aloud, probably the other

way too. It was used because it happened to be in the
family's luggage in Greece in the spring, when the reading began. The spellings in English of the Greek names
are not his, nor those of other contemporary scholars.
The non-Latinized forms will no doubt prevail some day
if books last that long, but for so personal an excursion as
this, the narrator had to opt for her lifelong pals Achilles
and Ajax, against the total strangers Akileus and Aias.
Alienation was too high a price to pay for linguistic logic.

E.C.

Eyes, Etc.

Try first to write a page a day this way. Get used to it. Other people have—Thurber et al. How strange it is that I fairly often forget what has happened and get shocked back into awareness of it, over and over, each time as if it were a brand-new circumstance. So the misery stays fresh and violent, when not obliviated, in that curious closet I seem to have built for it.

It stays there—shy wicked chameleon beast—even as I ruminate more or less all day, like a cow on its cud, over other people's worse sufferings. Type by type, name by name, many of course being known cases, mixed with the various mass horrors we take in by report. If we do take them in. Must get back to that some time—what we privileged ones as we're called (and are, oh yes!) ever do know of war, famine, torture etc. As if it weren't hard enough to consider the widows and others whose phone numbers you know by heart, the bereaved parents, the friends struck by some nightmare disease—the body going like a rotten apple as they observe, unless it's the mind the worm is in.

Their faces parade in the kitchen sink, over the bed you still for some reason make each day—everywhere, all day, an invasion, like ants. Slap one dead, never mind its juice on your fingers, there'll be ten more. All the time you're thinking which is worse, and how do they stand it, and why. Idiot gloom, not even playing at empathy. That it is not. It also serves no purpose, for them or you. Just a question of thinking who you are luckier than. For God's sake. That would be most of the world's population, wouldn't it?

Still, if so, what of it? You were following the obits anyway the last few years. It's normal to congratulate yourself when somebody younger than you kicks off, especially suicides. Moral as well as genetic superiority there. But keep on the track, my friend, if friend we can be to ourselves in such extremity. You're afflicted now. You've got to cope or decide not to, isn't that so? Then stop denying it, in your sneaky way. Open that closet. Face the facts.

Bullshit as the children say. And by the way, "cope" is a viler word than that nowadays. Very rapid diseases of language in our time; from which thought I deduce that biological and social maladies, since they so quickly link up in the head, must be part of the same subject. At the moment the warning I had in mind was just to watch the Pollyanna syndrome: sweet little me, so brave, better off than so many others, would gladly trade, give, something. Would NOT. Am NOT. This is HELL—out of the blue too (ha ha)—any worse, you wouldn't be hearing this much squeak out of me. Fact remains, does it not, I have extraordinary blessings to count, yes indeedy. Can walk, talk, cook. Have love, and loving lovely family—no goons or cult-cranks or other disasters there. Am not lonely or hungry or mistreated by anybody I know of, and can still dial the telephone if it's the shape I know, not one of those nasty new square push-button jobs.

Lapse there, a week or so. Things crawl along in
some sort of development—good or bad, hard to tell; such
matters seem to be up for redefinition, like everything
else. Finding-cause-for-cheer-in-spite-of-it-all, or breaking
into cheer without cause—like hives—hard to put down.
And why want to, you might ask. Why not just be grate-
ful for such a constitution, habit of pleasure in life, or
whatever. Because it's senseless, under these conditions;
idiotic; that's why. Like (*just* like?) neurotic depression I
never could understand or feel much sympathy for, God
forgive me. One hears of a lot of cases and I've known a
few. Funny? Is suicide funny? Well, ignoble anyway and
that's always partly comical, n'est-ce pas? Difference of
kind more than degree perhaps in ignobility; whiners
about life easier to see as funny than Ganelon and other
big traitors who do more obvious harm, cause deaths etc.,
and of course it's pathological to smirk at that or love and
glorify it like Genet (that fool Sartre, calling him Saint!).
But the whiners and certainly suicides may do as much or
more real harm, while remaining potentially absurd. The
Sylvia Plath virus now going around is surely as silly, i.e.
laughable as Rev. Moon et al. I can't feel either as particularly pathetic, though undoubtedly they are, especially if
everybody is seen as victim of outside forces, parents,
society and all that, which in fact leaves nothing but
pathos anywhere.

I digress. How nice. Didn't use to allow myself much
of that, thought it a defect, of brain or character. A fat
person eating candy. And so it is.

Another thing to watch out for: "What difference does

it make now," no question mark. Betty S. and all the
others with terminal this and that, lungs mainly, smoking
cigarettes like crazy, like hooked teen-agers. And why
not? Will get to that. There must be a reason, of some
Ethical Culture type. Anyway I feel there's a reason and
take that as evidence, true-believer fashion. However, am
still smoking myself, am holding a cigarette right now and
not bothering to argue that it's not lungs in my case. The
doctor won't quite say it's just as bad, or any better either.
There are certain hints and suggestions—meaning they
don't know, and on this particular point nobody is trying
to find out. Funds lacking probably, maybe interest too.
Imagine. Here we are this week with all those marvelous
instruments snooping around on Mars—Mars! war god!
we've been getting a lot of him in the Iliad, under the
name of Ares of course, and how upset he was by his own
half-mortal son's death—and right here at hand is this
catastrophe to a little living organism called ME and they
politely wash their hands of it, although no eleven-month
journey, twenty-two round trip, is needed to look into it
and there's no question as to existence of life in it. None
at all. I breathe, I laugh, with a little caution can even run,
and it costs them no billions, not a red cent, to get the
phenomenon under their cameras. Come here, Mars, they
say, and off I go at my own or our own expense, good
little planet-puppy, to this hospital and that, wherever
they say. Not that they're all fools or s.o.b.'s by any
means. You hear about such doctors but mine have been
dears, darlings, the kind who inspire confidence as the
saying goes—good kind people, probably bright too.
They just don't know. About me and all those others.
Which others? how many? who are they? how many stars
on the way to Mars? Oh, those *others*. What a crux and
puzzle they are suddenly. Their light and meaning and

places in the firmament are all different. It can't have happened overnight. I was too stricken at first; would cry when alone in the house, after having no reason to cry for twenty-four years. Or only one time and not for the old kind of reason then. Rather interesting experience, that slithery sort of wetness down the cheeks, not like any other water, more like new snakeskin I imagine when the old one has just been wrestled off against some good rough bark. Just a guess of course; I've never caressed a snake that I can remember, in any age of skin. N.B.: something to try, now that novelty is the order of the day—?

Who says? I mean, yes, everything's different, that's for sure, so call it novelty, but who says you have to accept it, experience it, still less relish it? Well, that's possibly the whole point—that and those tricky baffling *others* in the new layout. Will get back to it in due course, if there is such a course.

Right now must get back to that neurotic cheerfulness I left back there, which other people find admirable or at least say they do. Noun: fortitude. Adjective: stoic (noun too), stoical, both commonly misused. Will have to ferret out fortitude, and another newcomer—normalcy. Be careful. Digression may be restful as I was saying, after so many years of discipline, but to tell the truth it's just the vice I always thought, of both brain and character. Normalcy doesn't belong on this page but I'm liable to forget and it's important—though I believe this misfortune has made me less, not more forgetful. It would be in line with that false cheer to think so but it might be true. In case it's not I note the concept of normalcy and why it figures —because I might remember the word and not what matters about it. Also any benefit to memory from these unnatural conditions might be temporary, not to be counted on. So take all precautions possible, such as keeping kitchen utensils exactly where they belong, not relying on memory of having put one somewhere else last night. The very old must have to learn such habits, and with different applications (poems known, memories of love or political history, significant names or numbers) people in forced labor camps and such—gulag places.

Those OTHERS again. It's not time for them yet. I swear I'll get to them but it's not time. Am not ready. No, I didn't mean to say that, would hate to admit it, I meant it would be self-indulgent here; messy. It's not time in the sense of form.

What I was getting at, only as a notation, was normalcy. Not a notion I ever gave a bean about before so must hurry and explain before it slips into the crawl-space again, where incidentally there are a few snakes, more than last year I think but not poisonous.

It came in, normalcy that is, from a climatologist's remarks in the paper the other day. I never heard of a climatologist before but these new breeds crop up all the time—an ologist for everything. I'm becoming one myself, an expert on misfortune, eligible for a degree in same. Well, he said that what we of the last century or so have considered normal weather is not that at all. We've been spoiled rotten is the idea, and he has lots of dates and other data to prove it. We feel badly treated by droughts, floods, too hots and too colds etc. because we and our grandparents, I forget how far back, have lived through a spell of abnormal decency weatherwise. We just have no idea what this planet can perpetrate when it gets back to normal.

Of course I was an ideal recipient of that piece of scholarship, being the type quick to leap at analogy. It's obvious that the idea of normalcy in human life that some of us lucky ones grew up with—but never mind pounding it in. I just said it was obvious, didn't I? I admitted it. So don't ask me to kick myself for having cracked and splintered under this lightning bolt. God damn it it was news, unprecedented and intolerable as Jonathan Edwards said of the Last Judgment it so strongly resembles (really he said unavoidable and intolerable, less apt here). Only I thought—perhaps still think, will have to mull over that—that I had not, repeat not, earned it by any wickedness. Flaws anybody'll admit if pressed and some if not, it's their defect: "I'm so terrible," "I'm so envious . . ." I may have been a bit flesh-proud, I can see that now, a little stuck-up about health and strength and energy, but that shouldn't warrant any such castigation. In my humble opinion a rap on the knuckles would be enough. I was just disclaiming any wickedness beyond the normal. And so there we are back to you, alien idea, nuisance, interloper. Go away; get under there with the snakes. I'm sick of you. I want to enjoy my pain.

Like hell. I meant like hell I do but OK, take it the other way—this hell, so oddly lacking in physical pain, so quiet, decorous, almost beneficent you could say. Enjoy it? Well, I suppose a person might pay to be crazy; from some things that would be relief. But am not there yet, nor even considering it. Am not crazy, ergo do not enjoy what is not just unenjoyable but way over the other end of the scale. To hell with normalcy—tragic, piddling, dreary, whatever the humanologists want to call it.

I just want to understand what's happening. Those fits of cheer, those new crawling Others—no, not new but they didn't use to come through the floor this way, as though expecting to be caressed.

By the way, another topic to take up after a while: how to kill time. Very important.

Phone call from Mike F.'s—well, widow of sorts, though they'd been apart for a year—to say 1) she's getting married again, and 2) their little girl, going on two and a half now, who was with him and was thrown in an alley when he was killed by the mugger in New Haven last year, has permanent brain damage. Nothing to be done. Will have to be in an institution. It's almost the anniversary of his death and he had been here with the baby just before, the Irish in him still going strong; actually that was a couple of generations back but the wit and grin and long upper lip were right off the boat. Ex–bad boy and dropout and adventurer in South America, drifted into the family during a hitch as student but mainly that winter in France when his wallet and guitar had been stolen. Best thing ever happened to him, I mean losing the guitar; he was so terrible on it, he could have been arrested for musical indecency. Later all of a sudden was making it through law school, top of the class. Don't know why she felt the need to phone. We never got to know her well. Different Irish type—a year ahead of him in law school, lady ward-heeler you'd have said once, clearly aiming to be the first U.S. female President. Had figured she'd get there better without him, apparently. He was working ferociously himself the last years but did read poetry and do other things not useful by her lights, like putting himself out and very far out for people in trouble. And then all that comic armor he had—the Don't Touch Me, more than Homer's warriors wore; must have woken himself up laughing. I expect she thought that wouldn't get them places either, wasn't sincere; she was big on sincerity, a word I'm quite sure we never heard him use. Cute-looking though, a redder redhead than he, and kittenish in the beginning; he was nuts about her.

So we reel again under that blow, his friend David Y. too who happens to be visiting this week. A little younger than Mike, twenty-five or six now. Saying last night he would give anything to go to Mars. The pictures reminded him of certain beaches after a storm. I remarked that he didn't seem to have quite the training required. He said they ought to start sending people who could convey the experience, "poets or something"—and he will evidently be a good poet. He said all those poor astronauts can say is "Wow! it's beautiful! . . ." True. I said it might be hard to get back and then he surprised me, as there is certainly nothing S. Plathish about him, he has a good tough hold on life, as bartender, night watchman etc. has taken some nasty violent incidents in stride. "I wouldn't mind that. I really wouldn't. I'm just dying to go there." Said it in a very genuine, untheatrical way. Mike used to find him jobs, lend him money when he had any; I doubt if either had a closer friend.

But those other Others; all children of grief and woe naturally, that's why they're here. Older, bona fide widows for one bunch, as far as eye can see. Like Daddy's story of the man showing a moose at a western country fair, five cents a ticket, a quarter for a family ticket. A very ancient man with a tremendous white beard asks for a family ticket. Behind him is a great crowd of old people bent over with canes, then a mile or so of middle-aged and after them a still longer line of young couples with babies, on to flocks of children way off across the plains. All his family. "And way out there too?" "Yup." The dialogue goes on. "You can come in free. It's worth more to my moose to see your family than it is to your family to see my moose."

The widows come in, and widowers, less of a crowd but as large in loss, some of them, and those tortured by living love or lack of it. The moose is not interested, in them or me. How various their sufferings. Some of those left stunned by death have lost no more than the habit of piddling annoyance or a victim at hand, but if that made up all of life the loss is awful. Or so much more—never mind, everybody knows. No, nobody knows, even if you're the bereaved as it's called that's the only one you know; yourself. Bereaved—undertakers' word. Funny those Indians (East, but which?) used to burn the widow on the pyre, not the widower. Just economics of course, nothing to do with the sick soul, so perhaps sick was considered the healthy way to be. No great value to life and all that, supposed to be so different from our way of seeing it. I wonder if they (who they? usually taken to mean all Orientals) really think us as infantile as they're said to. And if we are, as on climate.

Novelty; obits; springtime of loss, grief, death of desire, death to be desired. As new as next year's row of hyacinths (the pink ones small and pale last April, must remember to do something for them).

The nightingale sang all night in the pension garden in Geneva. I cried. We came through that one.

Then another western plainful, or say the Sahara jampacked, standing-room only (I only saw the edge of that desert, one of many regrets; must make a list, if you can't kill time you can at least hurt it badly). They too can see the moose free and he still won't bat an eye. Parents of dead children; if they loved them truly, as truly as they knew how. Oh yes there can be impurities, but I'm not thinking of them, nor of any a priori rockbottom setup where the norm is despair. Children of promise; nothing wrong; I think of three who had serious talents, character, gaiety. Maybe they stole once from a supermarket, on a bet or out of loneliness, to keep in with bad company— the fine-grained do suffer the worst, in adolescence; nobody could say they had done anything evil or ever would have in their lives, outside our general margin of error. One cannot bear to look as their mothers and fathers come in, nor at those born defective, and their parents.

And the others. And still others. In wheelchairs; with their minds deliquescing. John M. eight years in perfect clarity of mind watching his nerve-ends decay. Couldn't feed himself finally. Asking, "What books would you read in my situation?" Couldn't hold one or keep it propped up. Not my case.

Pickers through garbage cans. Sleepers in doorways. I know them. They are talking to me. Because of my trouble of course; puts me in their camp. On pretty crummy grounds, some would think; they'd say I have no right to claim their society. However, long before the present disaster, I did hear the nightingale in the ramshackle garden in Geneva, singing for or in spite of musty velour parlor and three-story stairwell with dome of 1890 stained glass. A lot of dark yellow oak. No meals, just breakfast, though that one terrible evening, the hospital room not yet available, they did bring up tea and some sort of mangled egg on a tray, not unkindly.

If you think that company I've been mentioning makes me feel superior, guess again. Some people do call it empathy or sympathy and pride themselves on it. Bad stuff. Myself, to my credit let me say, where so little credit seems appropriate at the moment, I don't feel glad or sorry or anything that I can detect, about my new associations. *Je constate,* that's all.

One way to be useful to society: keep out from underfoot. This apropos of novelty, which in fact it may not come under at all but thinking about it certainly does. Plain time-killing doesn't serve so well. More effective, therefore useful, to imagine you're doing something, like this. When young I used to think if everything else was lost I'd go work in a leper colony. Now what kind of young girl's flight of fancy was that? Morbid, Mother would have said, so I never told her. Also was haunted by lonely spinsters, there seemed to be so many; as a shape of life enthralling, terrifying. "Even owl calls howling from the woodland/ Leave whole the silence patterns of the mind." That howling's a howler, can't be right; it was supposed to be a poem and I think I called it "The Farmer's Daughter"; she never married. Juvenile dread does make for lousy verse but needs to be recorded just the same, being probably the root of all later attitudes and assumptions. But why that particular dread? For bugaboos you'd think a disagreeable husband would be more like it. Not to me. I never imagined that. It was just a big long shape of Nothing I was afraid of. Creeping deterioration; senseless time. (Oddly enough, that farmer's daughter is blind in the last stanza.) But no, there's something more to that grim image as it comes back to me now, must try to get hold of it, as being connected some way with—ah, grandiose!—Philosophy.

I forgot to ask our philosopher friend the other night if he considered his métier—discipline they say now, another word I'll have no truck with, I wonder when it came in—in any case, if he thought of philosophy as in any way bearing on the will to live in adversity. I suppose he'd have to say yes of course, but I doubt it. I mean to the extent of its doing anybody any good. I think they keep their brainy games separate from even their own arthritis, like children playing Kala or Monopoly: all those pretty beans and printed slips that keep getting spilled on the closet floor. In our house only an occasional young visitor ever plays with them any more, yet I go on, I suppose a shrink would say compulsively, picking them up and sorting them. Another way of keeping out from underfoot, so useful; I don't honestly think I enjoy the annoyance at whoever spilled them but it's hard to tell about that sort of thing. Philosophers seem to have a great time flaying the spillers and untidiers of their game-pieces, probably get so wrapped up separating blues from reds and 5's from 10's they wouldn't notice the sky falling on them. But that's a surmise. I want to stick to what I know.

Come to think of it though, I did have another philosopher friend once, at least that's what he was professor of. He wouldn't have claimed more than that— not like those teachers of science and history who call

themselves scientists and historians. Good old Bailey.
Only he wasn't the type for college reunions where they
talk like that. Must have been around fifty when the
canoe rather suspiciously dumped him in Lake Michigan.
Drunk possibly; I never heard if the family had any idea.
Good man. So ugly and kind, too sensitive for that business. Always at sea with his emotions, loyalty (to wife) vs.
what he called "communication." That word really
opened vistas to him; he'd just discovered it, invented it,
when he was making me the confidante of his wild adoles-
cent, and unrequited but that didn't seem to matter,
amour in Paris, for an American girl his daughter's age.
Beet-faced, sow-bellied, all adimple, the beerglass-thick
spectacles alight with a sixteen-year-old's first utter, unut-
terable illumination of love. It drove him for the month
of May out of Philosophy into Creativity, another pent-
up yearning, and in two weeks while the girl was away
he wrote about two hundred pages of a novel, as he called
it. About that experience of course, pouring gallon-jug-
fuls of real life over the pages as non-writers always do
when driven to inflict themselves on that art form.
Clumsy brutes, they should compose music instead, it
would be over sooner. But he never meant to publish it,
he can be forgiven.

So ecstasy and anguish may make for rather similar
outpourings, is that it?

Oh shut up, Snidey, go change your skin, I could hear
you rattling a mile off. Nobody's talking about any novel
here, especially not a non-fiction one. A self-comforter,
that's all I'm in condition to aim for right now. What's
more my exalted friend had had no practice in that business, none whatever; it wasn't his line of work. Once I
avowed my ignorance in what was—philosophy, not

belated rapture—and he said ever so pleasantly, really meaning it as a compliment, that I didn't need it. I was always extra fond of him for that, since I agreed with it. Then back to home, job, loyalty, in the flat country, and after a few years the overturned canoe. The word "communication" was just then beginning to be taken over by the advertising business; that may have been what killed him. I hope the "novel" had been burned.

He had written it in a room at the Hotel Lutétia, Gestapo HQ not so long before, where a young French couple I had known were subjected to one of those acts that made World War II a new kind of dividing line in our family history. How wholesome and decent all the killing in the Iliad is, after all. Man to man, nothing sneaky, rules known, above all, genuine virile anger however babyish that may be. No psychos. No Hotel Lutétia. And the will of the gods for sure comfort, however silly they might be and clearly were, in Homer's mind too. His only comic characters. But to be revered at the same time, I wonder how literally; a very sly job. From them, with all their foibles and deceits and infantile exercise of power, comes dignity to the fallen and whatever comfort there may be for their families.

Like Christian will of God, *come Dio vuole* and all that. Yes, Religion does it, this is where it really comes in first. Philosophy is a children's game, forget it, teaches nothing but the use of your wits to go round the board and defeat an opponent. Only Religion tells you how to stand the blows of fate, and oh Lord give us the sense to envy only the true believer, nobody else. That's not altogether fair. The Greeks a few hundred years later did work out some really quite useful and usable philosophy, to keep your cool with while drinking hemlock and so on. But they're

the first and last, the Greeks, never happened again. All
those German windbags, construct-mongers, mouth-
ing and blustering, making their little-boy castles of hot
air.

No, no, for God's sake—speaking for us afflicted of the
earth (snicker there in the wings, from some of that company I was talking about) give us Religion every time. I
can't go so far as to ask to believe in it, but that's just a
matter of temperament and my bad luck.

Snicker, I meant, at the nerve—my putting myself in
their class, presuming to move in their set. Like a matter
of yachts. Ours is a lot grander than yours, costs more to
maintain too. As if it were my fault I wasn't born rich in
infirmity and sorrow and never happened to acquire
much along the way, until now. OK, I'm a beginner in
their field (discipline?) but they should be charitable. I'll
agree to be a non-resident member of the club but I'm in,
whether they snub me or not.

However, they could have smirked that time for various other reasons, as that widows are often merry—so the
waltz tells us—and often just plain relieved, once they get
used to the new arrangements: the second coffee cup not
to be put out, the toilet seat never found up. Referring to
those too old or well-bred to acquire other gents in a
hurry. (Mostly hearsay report; in my own acquaintance-
wide poll it would have rather a low percentage rating.)
And spinsters are bygone, absolutely. No such animal.
They're in singles bars or something, God knows, anyway
no owl calls for them. Rock racket, group sex, advertise
for a playmate in the N.Y. Rev. of Books. For true long-
time faithful lovers the brook murmurs all night and
when death does them part they carry their grief high in
honor like a basket of laundry on a peasant woman's head.

Ablution. Laundry. Bad thoughts and other sins to be

washed out regularly, with no more thought about it than
in dipping the finger in holy water by the church door,
to make the sign of the cross with. Lucky they who can
honestly do it. The washer-dryer a great deprivation.
Shirts and sheets playing in breeze and sunlight on the
line, lovely banners, in motion and function so like angels'
wings, they might be the origin of the idea. The fresh
start is always an illusion but a necessary one.

David Y. not so tough after all. Seems he recently got
as far as head in the oven and gas on. Drunk maybe. So
that is the nature of his interest in going to Mars. He left
today, and I feel a little apprehensive for him. But now
suppose such a friend—or one's own child!—were one of
those kooks his age, the middle-class young men we've
been reading about this week, who kidnapped the busload
of children in California. What do you make of that,
Moose? I do wish you could tell.

Last night, three new records, a present—Brahms clarinet quintet and two contemporary works, one a snappy
setting of asinine words as so often happens. Brahms no
favorite of mine, either symphonies or piano galopades;
this clarinet work might be something else. But ears churl-
ish about music lately. I pretend to listen. Also last night,
earlier, that overpowering scene of Achilles' immortal
horses, gift of Zeus to his father Peleus, standing still with
their heads drooping to the ground, as they weep, literally
shed tears, over the death of Patroclus. By chance it fell
to beautiful dark-eyed Alice B., rocked by divorce and
daughter's death in car crash three years ago, to read that
passage. She was glad it had not been one of the slaughter
lists before and after—"Like a football game," so many
have said; "a boys' book." They can't have read it; wrong
on many counts. The fastidious detail of each killing itself
conveys a transcendence. And the will of the gods tran-

scending their human foolishness—some grand solidity of belief there after all. Then most beautifully, after those horses' tears, Zeus's lovely meditation as he pities them in their grief, wishing he hadn't given them to Peleus and condemned them to "ache" so for the fate of poor mankind, although themselves immortal. "Poor things ..." Nothing, he says, is so sad to look on as human beings.

What a marvelous switch, after you've been disliking him so in his caprice—insane autocrat, an Idi Amin—and surely the early hearers of the story must have thought so too, only they would know the rest of it. We say to ourselves, why doesn't he stop the damn war if he's so almighty, and they knew better. That he couldn't, is really no king of anything but only the immutable laws of our chancy lot, and suffers as much as any mortal over the misery he seems to inflict.

Evening of bright cheery talk around the table, this time on sorry to tragic underpinnings. Three matres dolorosae in the house last night, a father and stepfather too but male disappointment in children, however lethal, is more a blow to the windpipe than a wound. The Pietà is Mary's mourning, for reasons more standard than immaculate conception. But no Christ-figure here, even if one or two have put on a replica of Veronica's veil in their patchwork wanderings. One dead, yes, in this roll call— Alice's twelve-year-old daughter—and one who would do better to be, Marcia by name; it would be gross hypocrisy to put it more charitably, no matter what half-submerged violences (there certainly were some) strained the home in her childhood.

In that case the couple are spending the night, instead of driving rather a long way home as planned, because Marcia is there for a wonder—no, for the usual reason: money, for a new cult or motorcycle or trip to the Himalayas—and the mother, normally so composed, is a wreck on arrival. We've never before seen her drink too much. Our son and the kindly doctor stepfather, her husband for ten otherwise happy years, have to carry her downstairs, to vomit and to bed. The once darling daughter had been twisting her arm for cash, as if there were much handy, and threatening and reviling her all weekend. The other couple, old friends, have stopped over en route to their summer cabin in Canada. Fat, bald, witty historian, acerbic to the core; the only statue of grief he could model for would be far from Renaissance—a couple of razor blades in some vital recess or intestinal coil would be most like it. Yet close-tied husband and wife are, by the same now-chronic incredulous dismay over a creature they did not spawn—adopted, that one, perhaps a few months too late, damage irreversible. Still, a cut above Marcia, the loudest, the ringleader of the unseen ones at the table, who have made themselves the diners and us their meal.

Black leather eyelashes to match her pants; screwing with anything that comes down the pike; jailed a dozen times, California, Europe, all over, and Ma and the good-natured stepfather get the best lawyers, psychiatrists etc. or used to. At a top-flight art school one year—in the art easiest to debase into catch-all and crutch, poor Photography—her thesis was what you'd expect, Polaroid series of her own genitals. Did hitches at bombing and drug-running, now says she wants managerial job in the fashion world, wouldn't consider anything menial. Our friend, a good if small-gauge sculptor, used to welcome this child, and love and hope, and contrive for the sister and brother at least to be friends. Now she only wishes she would stay away, vanish, be to them as though never born. Or no, of course there can be no such only; that is what she must and does try to wish.

We ourselves are half dazed by this unprecedented crossing of stars in our house. The many younger people we know well, ages five to thirty-five let's say, are nobody's xerox copy but aren't spinning in black space either. They're delightful, and courageous; they're great; would happily adopt any one or all fifty. Of course they can't all be supershiners like the three Garner children but—

Letter from Arthur T. today (will get back to the Grieving Mothers) saying, along with sympathy for my plight, that we have to learn to grow old. Quotes nice piece of Chinese wisdom to that effect. (Ah but I'd been howling all this time, I'm *not* old, nowhere near *that* old, and come from long-lived people, was counting on at least twenty more good years, thought I would learn to some small degree the tricks of my trade.) His beloved Polly, he writes, has had brain damage from her open-heart surgery a couple of years ago (I didn't know it could do that) and has lost I don't know just what of her faculties but her flute-playing, for one thing, and wonderful memory for music are gone. We were in college at the same time.

Yes, we must learn. I don't know what, or how, or why. We must. Something. It set me back hard. Ashamed? I don't know. Shame can be self-indulgence too.

Count your blessings, so many people say, meaning not

offspring per se—that would be a laugh, it could be another Marcia—but our darling specific Prodge and Ennie who happen to be here this long lovely summer of such exquisite pain—adjustment I suppose it's called. And oh I do count them, one two one two, all the livelong day, and confess though it's the out thing this year to having sung praises unto Nature and the goddess Fortune for every day of their lives, and make finger-signs of a Sicilian sort against the banana peels that life could strew on their steep paths. They run so fast, they aim so far, they never look. This business has made everything precarious. Must control that. Of course we would wish for them never to grow old, that's only natural and another aspect of the gods (Homeric) that makes good sense. That some beings at least be imagined as we would want to imagine our children—alive, young and beautiful forever. Takes some of the curse off what's called being down to earth. The Grecian Urn syndrome. But scratch that reference. Things are bad enough without Keats dying at twenty-five.

Nothing uncommon, though, about parental pride and joy, parlous times and reports to the contrary notwithstanding. If the Garners weren't dotty about their brood, they'd be daffy, just for one pair of parents out of the many that swarm to mind. Only this kind doesn't make news, or apparently suit the computer's stomach either so they don't even make the statistics. All-round rightness and brightness and fun, in spite of all the wicked world can do; in the brochure it would say "you name it." No brochure; no story, even though in the case of the young G.'s, ages fifteen to twenty now, along with more ordinary excellences, in school, sports, music, it would have

been plain to anybody in Homer's time that both Apollo
and Aphrodite had had a finger in the pie, somewhere,
somehow, and that would seem noteworthy. No slur on
those serene, companionable parents, hard-working
teachers both, with a streak of adventure and daring that
can verge on madness and stop, triumphant—disaster
averted, good time had by all. More likely the gods for
once just chose to reward that innate grace, and Apollo's
gift was a singularly pleasant one. The three children's
voices in everyday speech are so agreeable—low without
being hoarse or husky, and naturally melodious—it
would be a pleasure to hear them even if they had nothing
much to say. They do have, plenty, and very good and
engaging talk it can be—they're all big readers—but I've
never heard one of them monopolize or butt into a conversation. I forget if delicacy, or tact, of that sort is in
Apollo's province or some other.

Well now just a minute, hold your horses, you're beginning to bore me with these paragons whoever they are.
I don't wonder the computer spits them out. They can't
be real; you've got to be lying. Bad eggs, rotten times,
that's what the computer likes to hear, because it's true,
ask any sociologist. Anything for a high, gotta find myself, primal scream, audience participation, right-on methodology, latest gimcrack in Zen or any other kook cult
some smart guy's making a pile out of, and where's the
money coming from? Momma and Poppa, that's who, all
their fault anyway. Who's lolling on the Spanish Steps in
Rome, arms blotched from needles? who broke into your
house in Connecticut last year?—son of a local minister
one of them was. Face it. Get in the swim, and listen—

No, I was not lying. The G.'s have a cabin a few miles
away they come to often, more in winter as they're all

wonderful skiers. I'll introduce you some time, although as I said they're not all that unusual except in physical beauty, male and female. And thanks a lot but I wouldn't ask a sociologist the time of day or how to get to the nearest gas station; for a long time nobody knew how to describe what those people are and do, so the expression "don't know from nothing" had to get invented. But I think your trouble is worse, and I don't mean just being a lush on statistics and melodrama. It's perfectly clear that you've never heard of Apollo, or Aphrodite either—a very dangerous lacuna, one that people have been known to fall into in the dark, never to be heard of again. You really should bone up on them, immediately.

Still, I have to admit that the young ghosts at the table, although all vegetarians, were making mincemeat of us without a qualm. Their own parents seemed to be used to it but for us outsiders it was a queer sensation, being ground by teeth and gulped down gullets that weren't, in a manner of speaking, there. Quite a few of these hungry presences there were too—a number of subsidiary off-spring and semis and steps on one side or another that a novelist would have to go on about. Between them they would pretty well bear out most of the sociological tirade refuted above. No murderers in this lot anyway, or mur-derees either so far, and several, I hear, are rather sweet-natured in their aimlessness, or pursuit of aims beneath the intelligence of a rabbit. Personally, excepting Marcia, I'd feel worse having a national pollster in the family.

Conversation, as we disintegrate, is lively, general, amusing, in the glow from the old hanging table-lamp, kerosene once upon a time—a sweet lamp I must say, must consider it further. The third mother has recovered and come back to the party, hair no greyer and untidier than

flesh, a tattered Vlaminck, but with her good wits in
order. Her first husband, the semi-eminent art critic, left
their home when Marcia was twelve to shack up with a
young black man, unemployed by rock bands and later
indicted for trying to kill him, but that's not her problem.
For all the mothers, the thing is to keep something back
from the repast. The struggle shows in a certain by now
habitual tension of eye muscles and rocklike set of jaw in
any moment of listening or other silence, the bone structure of all three faces being remarkably fine and strong.
It would be, quickly after a laugh or remark, as if some
great cave-mouth had snapped shut, allowing something
inside to claw and cavort unseen. Anecdotes, precedents
and possibilities, illustrations to the point, smiles, laughter;
decent feelings, well-stocked minds. What went wrong?
what went wrong? Sounds like angry lions and tigers in
those rock caves, and then all of a sudden—oops! watch
the wineglasses—it's a waltz that has broken out, strings
coming in heavy, rhythm irresistible, children clapping
their hands and jumping with excitement—which a
minute ago was all from the bullfrog playing bassoon by
the pond and the lazy half-moon drifting over—and
grown-ups all about to leave their places and dance, un-
mindful of the missing chunks of their anatomies. But that
too subsides, and in the few seconds before talk resumes
we hear the soul-provoking four-note admonition of our
friend the great owl down across the brook.

The lamp has a white porcelain shade with a glass shade
inside that, fitting around the wick and held by the four
little brass upright prongs, and with the somewhat ornamented glass bowl bottom that used to hold the kerosene.
Still does if some electrical part goes bad. We don't bother
when it's just the power off. More brass, no, gilt wrought

iron, for the also ornamented holding frame and chains to the ceiling, which give a foot or two of play up and down depending on how intimate you want to feel and what hidden recesses of mind and spirit are in jeopardy. It was just that nothing in the progeny in question had turned out as hoped. And what exactly had been hoped? That wars were over, population stable, whales multiplying, the chainsaws not screeching all day in these beautiful woods for the benefit of developers? Well, yes and no—they weren't that unrealistic surely, nor are they mercenary. No rat-racers, no money-freaks, in that group.

Then a fragment of answer struck me, as Alice so beautifully sang Ravel for us—of the three dolorosae the most akin to Mary, who for all we know may also have had some flibbertigibbet strain antedating her child's awful death, quirks of character dropped away in legend, as now from our friend through her voice. Singing, she rises and lifts us all toward what used to be seen as a throne, beyond personality.

The discovery was, not of what went wrong—wouldn't want to make the computer feel unneeded—but what *is* wrong. That particular bunch of—My goodness, how extraordinary; our Number One national obsession and we haven't got a decent word in our language for them, no way to translate *les jeunes.* You can say "the problems of the young" if your mind works that way but "there were fifteen young at the table" would sound like a mistake in Chinese, and "young people" went out with the horsehair sofa. Hence in recent years that abominable "kids" for everything up to if not beyond middle age. Well, you know who I mean, and the amazing fact about the ones in question—here's my contribution to the Social Sciences, which have a good share of blame in the matter

—is that they *just can't read!* Oh, they can make out the words, but I mean read—Homer for instance, or history, or anything intelligent people for thousands of years have been willing to give an arm or a leg to have opened to them. (And I, what would I give to have it back again, for a week, for one day—?) Went to what's called the best schools, every one of them, and then this horrible disease hit them, must be a virus, and they never opened a real book again. Stood around laughing that day at the fire in Alexandria—oh yes, they were there; maybe even helped put the torch to the library.

Honk away, Moose. In the caverns not open to lamp-light are such as can outbellow you.

The lamp also has two crowns of the same dull-gilded iron, as if a small bear had had pretensions to king-ship and these were found later among his treasures. Their crude ornateness of design very pleasing because some-how demure, not overdone, of the same school and period as the old black kitchen range, wood-burning, that we have in the cabin. When not rusting away in some old cellar-hole, now junkheap in the woods where once were mowed fields and patches of cosmos and lupine by the kitchen door, these articles are terribly alive with an in-nate idea of dignity in the commonplaces of life, whether or not that would be upheld in any particular household or instance. The scrollwork as necessary as the metal handle for shaking the ashes down, or on the lamp the tiny brass disc, right size to hold between thumb and fore-finger, at the end of the lever for raising and lowering the wick. Food, family dinner, have simply got to be ritual is what they say, and these objects we depend on every day must carry their part of it, otherwise we'd go crazy with transience, or float around weightless in our rational kitchens like astronauts, rocketed free of all mental (spiritual?) gravity. A pot of African violets on the windowsill isn't enough to do the job, especially as they probably weren't grown from seed on the premises.

The two crowns fit together when the lamp is all the way up, but that makes a rather too diffused, unfriendly light, so generally they are far apart and you forget the top one, conversation and faces are so absorbing in the glow below. That's not too strong, with a 75-watt bulb it's just right, and without any of the ladylike penumbra of present-day candlelight, in which your fork goes robotlike over the plate, long-distance-directed, and is apt to come up with squash instead of beef, to the surprise of your teeth which were set for real work and may clack rudely as a result. Still worse is when the hostess, aware of those drawbacks, has left electric wall-lights on along with the candles, which then serve no purpose but to wistfully announce their gentility and the obligation on you to be worthy of it. Don't say shit or fuck at that table, for instance; not that you normally would but you do get a hankering to under these circumstances. None of that in the light we're discussing. It is, however, strong enough so people could notice the frayed lines in the red-checked oilcloth, and perhaps they do. I give them a thought once in a while myself but only in the morning. For company in Connecticut, out of some atavism or from having inherited the silver candlesticks, we go in for the combination described above so I could speak with authority—an expert on something at last.

Digression again? Don't be silly. The lamp is right at the

heart of all this; it matters extremely. What could be more precious, subject to fonder criticism now than light?—all light, even though it's not all "spent" and this is not, it's true, "ere half my days in this dark world and wide." It's a little later than that, but a day is a day. I want a light that tells something. I want to see! and still can pretty well, up to a point. Also to be considered, the execution-day phenomenon: flash of vision, they say, of your whole life which must mean life and times; they'd be hard to separate.

Furthermore, as Homer was born knowing, blind or not—very likely not, I'm told—to catch your story it's wise to circle around it, get it securely in the net once and for all. Just in passing, once and for all is a curious expression; would seem to apply to death exclusively but of course that's not so, Q.E.D.

It's also not true that cancer and crime and car accidents take only the finest of the young. You'd have to believe literally in the devil to think it. But it seems so. And from the written word, that passing fad, we know it seemed so always, when it was a matter of smallpox, diphtheria, unmechanized accidents.

So back to Religion, old bugbear. How else tolerate, if not explain, such ghastly injustice—improvidence too, for survival of the species—as that a Marcia lives and may well live a long time doing damage all the way, and Mike F., enhancer of life to so many . . . They were the same age—twenty-seven last year.

I locked the cat in here by mistake late yesterday, now she needs to go out and can't understand why I don't stop the rain. I am supposed to be able to do that. A drizzle she would brave but this is a downpour. I hold the screen door open to give her the impossible choice, she draws back puzzled and saddened and alternates between rubbing against me—to ingratiate me or comfort herself? perhaps both—and meowing piteously. I am The God That Failed, i.e. like all gods, according to Hoyle. Now she is all bunched up on her haunches, staring motionless through the bottom of the screen at the inimical element. I would love to know what she remembers of the two or three terrible adventures in her past, and the others we never knew about. I realize there are certain differences between her and me, even on a day like this. She's a skillful and shameless killer for one thing.

Must remember to get back to time-killing. That was a terrible adventure, for several months. Haven't yet got a perfect grasp of the subject. Or it might just be too unpleasant to dive into. You could get the bends. So we continue, the grey and white cat and I, to dree our weirds. (Looked that up the other day, I mean somebody did for me. "Weird" OK, meaning of course fate, as in adj. weird sisters. In dictionaries at hand no "dree." It could be crooning or weaving or just counting as with beads. Do wish I'd spent my time better when times were better, when there was time—and all that: the most boring human wail. But I mean it modestly. Just wish I had memorized a big dictionary.)

Rather sad days in ALS crowd (Alternative Life Style) hereabouts, on the whole quite admirable and peaceful, not like the bad scenes some places, even nearby towns. A few of our young Refugees from It All almost too straitlaced; drugs at peak never conspicuous right here; con-types and Buddhist-come-latelies just birds of passage, would get a house or other shelter for a while and soon vanish. But things aren't what they were. Flotsam and Jetsam are breaking up, after five years in their hilltop shack. Annabelle Lee, one of several with a fatherless child or two, is consumed by dislike of her latest consort and regret at not having gone to college. Lancelot, our Ph.D. (Comp. Lit.), is fed up clerking and haying for subminimal pay, and two or three ABD's (All But the Dissertation) have been caught in a sigh over the money and so-called higher professions they spurned. Want to grow our own food, work with our hands. Fine. But then after a few years this boredom, like sirocco, with no literal sea and desert for its route; something missing; what is this strange monotony? The family pickle, the common muddle, the world's weird, or maybe just interesting conversation—might they get to be missing? Some, the last year or two, contrive to let you know their fathers were college professors or successful businessmen, something that kept them off their uppers, i.e. not so long ago despicable. Too bad; such nice people; you wish you could help restore their conviction.

The real curse, hardest to admit, is the "creative" stuff. Society can absorb just so much pottery and hand-weaving even if fairly good, just so many yowls and daubs in the name of art. You need a whole different social setup, tradition, guilds, generally shared sense of form etc. to protect the untalented in those fields. Enthusiasm a most undependable substitute; quickly gives way to depression and laziness, then desperate scramble for cash to pay the shrink. Father help me, I want to do my thing, I've tried everything. Cobble shoes, try carpentering a while; drift, out of sight of the skills it's too late to acquire, until some group therapy gets you, "as a swallowed bait/On purpose laid to make the taker mad."

"Creative," though, that's a PTA word. It's some of the mothers now wringing hands I used to hear bandying it about, so what could they expect. Rich or middle, doesn't matter; the poor are something else. Ladies redoing the living room out of the shelter mags, busy with divorce number two or three, want the kids finger-painting. Let them choose themselves what other subjects, motivation is all, must not be made unhappy, Latin irrelevant. Etc. And the fathers, quite a few of them, with their lying crooked deals, even those not reeling off the bar-car five days a week, a fifteen-year-old runaway daughter in the East Village is about what they deserve. Or a shaved-pate son at Synanon, or studying Urdu without pay, or fag-whoring in the street.

Oh but stop—hush! this will never do! Homer, help! Are there no great deeds to sing in the mainstream of our glorious society? are not these very gents we've been roughing up among the doers of same?

There are; they are. We stand corrected and contrite. Must have gotten carried away by that last-ditch vision we were talking about. Have to watch out for that; if you get a reprieve you might have to live down some embarrassing opinions of your society and fellow humans, pro and con. It's risky getting too good a look at all that's to be loved and admired, and hated and deplored. Luckily, few live to tell about it.

Granted, it's not just a matter of individual capacity. That has to occur in an age conducive to it, to wit, Elizabethan or classical French drama or sculpture in Periclean Athens. Burst of national energy, releasing all sorts of improbable capabilities. So those fathers able or not to leave the bar-car at the right station are to be praised, but also seen as specimens of a wondrous time, sharing their glory with that creature now crawling over Mars and its nurses in Pasadena. Nixon and Co. couldn't have gone it alone; obviously needed a propitious climate and the one they had, and their ilk still have, was and is practically perfect. "I am not a crook." How that goes to the current national heart of things; greatest stroke of presidential wordplay since the Gettysburg Address. Of course he would have endeared himself to more people by avoiding the negative, or reversing it, as in "I am not ashamed to be a crook." But he made his meaning no less clear and doubletalk is an art in itself as well as a habit. You don't expect Rubinstein not to touch the keys when confronted with a piano.

So get out the rag and let's hear a tear. The land of the lie and the rip-off we finally have become. We've made it the norm. We've made it. Other countries doing as well or better don't concern us in quite the same degree. Alas, only the tiniest proportion of fancywork in our business world ever gets publicly celebrated. Big profit from neglect and abuse of the aged always a favorite; Gramp and Granny angle ("The horse knows the way/To carry the sleigh") makes it easier to grasp than the really big gambles on mass murder, chemical, nuclear, by manufacture of defective plane and car parts etc. But there are millions more of those wonderful men out there, and some wonderful women too, real Americans, who ought to be getting just as much of a hand. There are several plundering these woods right this minute, to the tune, along with the chainsaws, of bribes and lies enough to pave the whole of the Green Mountains, as indeed is the idea. The ski areas go from one swindle and scandal to another, all good clean business, nobody in jail yet; clean meaning the way everybody does it. The squawkers are just the little suckers who lost their life savings or the price of an A-frame or something—the holier than thou's, or the type who sickened and died on the way west in our glorious history. No room for them, it's every man for himself, better they catch a virus, a good mean one.

Plenty of skiers of that heroic stripe. It's stirring to ride the lifts with them, I don't mean those who engrave four-letter words with pole-tips or jackknives on the plexiglass, hard workers though those are, but the ones with broader interests, the right-thinking typical crooks, in business or politics. Even below private-plane level they always have something interesting to say. It's a confession box, best in the gondola to the summit; the others too short for meaningful revelation. No danger, they'll never see you again, you don't know their names and furthermore have on the same model Rossignols—now there's a bond; it might even turn out you drive the same make of car; that really brings people together.

Not that they usually come out with the real story of course, but priestlike you probe, between remarks on temperature and trail conditions and best routes to here or there. Nothing like talk at a cocktail party or anywhere else. Far subtler currents play round that little enclosed island-for-two, traveling up through dazzle, fog, or blizzard if you're both that hardy, where feet and volition alike are useless, and snow or ice (frozen granular it's called here) could as well be miles as yards below. Plane trips make for odd confidences too, same suspension of control over your fate for the time being, but there's a very different undertone to that, being cooped up with a lot of people and able to move around now and then. This tête-à-tête, or hip-to-hip, high above earth with a single stranger is unique. Not that getting a finger on the nation's pulse is all it might afford or does at all perhaps to many. But for a wife and mother blessed in love and luck so many years, and approaching if she only knew it the age of probable if not multiple adversity, that is exquisite lagniappe, to round off the deeper delights of such a day.

Lord what did I say there? Age, adversity—? The words bring the dog-howl to my throat, like six months ago. I never figured on that conjunction, always said old age must be graceful and generous like my grandmother's, without face-lifts, without loss of laughter except for a while after that other coffin closed in its own due time. Sure, hundreds of better skiers flew by, I admired, no reason to envy; was never a star, was doing about as well as ever and loving it, barring certain nasty days and patches and a couple of hitches on crutches. Figured I'd stop without regret some far-off day, when timidity got to outweigh pleasure. But I see now—those hateful words were needed. Good old discipline! crafty elf—and loyal! keeping my theme intact in spite of everything and even demanding a name for it. OK, I submit. The Anatomy of Affliction—will that do? or The Afflicted Anatomy. But my dear lady, you're only dealing with a physical disability, sudden and mysterious to be sure, but not very dire as such things go, not likely to be total (as in totaling a car) nor even involving any physical pain, furthermore occurring among those blessings that are so joyously to be counted. "Ghastly deprivation," "hideous handicap" say the letters from friends. I said, "But Doctor, what you're telling me is to me a lot worse than death." It was no lie. If you're totaled, does it matter if wheels and a fender are still good for scrap? Run along to the junkyard, get it over with. This knack I've been practicing, of keeping out from underfoot, as distinguished from pure time-killing in the first months, may not be all that dependable. Leaving brook, woods, hanging iron lamp when the leaves fall, may knock it into a cocked hat whatever that is—evidently something like broken pitcher or smashed VW. Question: in a question of killing time, can there be earlier and more recent months? Must reflect. Might lead to grasp of Theory of Relativity, or at least international dateline.

All right, dear elf, best friend, will this do for the moment, if moments there are? (Adrift—in space or time, geography or duration the same: the very sound is like a knell, now that it begins to tickle the outer edge of my understanding. Poor doped-up wandering young, who must spit on pity, else would give up altogether, for the first time I think I begin to feel for you in your stinking jeans and sleeping bags. Wild animals have their lairs and rigorous routes to travel. You don't even care if it was Denmark or Afghanistan or the Long Trail you slept on last night. You don't read, so it makes no difference; anywhere is nowhere. Adrift—I soon like you maybe, in my fashion, so much meaning eluding me. "The dolphin-torn, the gong-tormented sea"—why, only yesterday that was my small garden, my cabin door.)

Meanwhile, I was left sharing a much smaller cabin, open below the shins, with the lean, muskrat-eyed lawyer from New Jersey, middle forties or so, wife and kids in cars ahead, tension in speech and gestures merely chronic,

nothing to do with immediate circumstances with which
he has no particular quarrel. On the contrary, he's been
enjoying himself, he says, and is being as affable as his
rather tight and wary if not hyperventilated nature per-
mits. We talk about schools in Fort Lee. He cares a lot
about the best education for his children. Worried about
prevalence of drugs. Has other civic concerns, none too
emphatic but wouldn't oppose a good public library for
his town, if cost was kept in limits. Is not even rabid
against welfare, only against cheaters and stealers among
recipients, that burns him up. Is staying in one of the
middle-to-high-priced lodges, not the swankest; more often rents chalet. Also familiar with Vail, Alta, Garmisch
etc. but for a short break and with school and all what can
you do, this is all right, he's not complaining.

O saisons, ô châteaux! Did I ever abuse the heart's wild
intake of certain joy and wonder, a counterradiance, in all
that white-gold splendor as we glide heavenwards, God's
grandeur in shook foil around us past the screen of ob-
scenities—woods and packed slope of such different han-
dling in the brilliance, as unlike as hawk-skilled skiers
swooping are from the brute crashers-down or the simply
cautious or inexperienced who make their turns like
ferryboats—did I let love, of motion and bright air, be
more than was fitting, for it to lead to this far swifter
shadowing in? Not quite the passing over, the *trépas*, Rim-
baud brought his *bonheur* to, not just yet, but such a
squeeze and slowing. And not to ride again through the
sky with heroes, their minds racing even in vacation week
toward their marvelous plums and Iliums. Visions of
booty—gold bathroom fixtures, call girls—give Mercu-
ry's wings to their expensive yellow boots on the way
down.

The lift stopped, with us about halfway up, as is its
wont. Stayed stopped quite a while. Feet got cold. If
you're there with a loved one or equivalent you can rub
noses or breathe down each other's necks. I had guessed
long since, at least two minutes back, that the lawyer's
practice was not all in simple old-fashioned real estate.
Had had a thrilling intuition of the not quite aboveboard,
the more than meets the eye, the laundered payments, the
doctored books. At the second halt he said, laughing,
"This makes me feel better about not paying for my
ticket." Nobody in the family had, for the whole week,
nor the family of friends they were with, eight or nine
skiers in all. Had gotten away with it so far. More than
by God's sunlight on snowfields was I dazzled, frigid in
rockabye sway, to think of the bedtime or anytime pre-
cepts they must impart to their children, for whom public
schools were not good enough, you can see why. And
what if they got stopped in the line? "Oh I'll just say the
ticket's on my other parka, I left it in the lodge. Of course
I wouldn't do it to an individual but these big corpora-
tions . . ."

Another time it was the garment industry. You'd have
had to stand on your head to get that one. Young guy,
very down on ski-thieves especially those working for a
syndicate; all third-person, some little matter of a quarter
of a million and the company (subsidiary) bankrupted
while the perpetrator, the speaker himself if certain looks
and inflections didn't lie, sails on to bigger and better, as
then waving a cheerful goodbye he flew in well-schooled
parallels over the glazed rim of the canyon. Ajax, Di-
omedes, watch out! A new race of men of valor, skilled
in the use of weapons, No Holds Barred and Passing the
Buck the mottoes, cash the prize, has arisen to wipe your

names from human memory. Not that the names are
likely to be replaced in a hurry. The words we bards and
scribblers know—honor? shame?—don't seem to apply.
Dictionaries no help. Homer too had trouble conveying
the full power and glory of Achilles but had gods for
reference, no mean asset. Hephaestus working all night to
create (OK here) that wonderful shield, such as never
before heard of in the world, with all its scenes and characters, so it wouldn't be just a single hero however re-
markable but really all the meaning and density of life
that would go forth to battle—that gives you the idea. No
such supreme artist, or even a finger-painter that I know
of, sweats all night to honor any Chairman of the Board,
even multi-national. Makes it hard to do them justice.

Just to pass the time I told lawyer B (very high IQ,
acquainted with ancient term Morality, might even have
taken a course in it, job in some state atty. genl.'s office
if he wasn't the a.g. himself) about conversation with
lawyer A (from New Jersey, no lift ticket). Pile-lined flaps
and vizor down, mitt over long thin nose not often privileged to be so cold—two or three weekends a winter all
he could take from that important work—clacked his skis
together pensively, mystified by my having thought such
a thing worth mentioning. He let out a small icicle of a
sigh and said rather sadly, perhaps thinking of his mother
as one school of balladry prescribes in encounters with
harsh facts of life, "I don't think there *are* any honest
people any more. I never meet any. I guess I don't move
in the right circles."

Weep, Momma. Keep staring, Moose—no, I haven't
forgotten you, not for a minute. We came in free, for
your benefit. Now just one more in this category you

might enjoy. Hang in there, be patient. I know it's per-
verse to hate this one, out of so many, but I can't help it,
I do, every time I think of it. That's how contrary the
human animal is. All I actually saw this one steal was a
place in line or rather four, there being also his wife and
another toney couple he was playing Virgil to, getting
them in the ski-patrol door, right to the take-off point
instead of joining the fifty-minute trudge with us sinners.
Perfect spring Sunday, longest lines ever. The first chair
he swiped, having overawed the attendant with his air of
authority, was about to be sat in by a boy around fourteen
and his mother, regulars, with season passes. The boy was
a beautiful skier, I'd seen him often, and must have been
incensed after the long wait, but all he said was, quietly,
"How come?" The tycoon or whatever he was, anyway
Groton-toned gent above average height and way above
average apparel and equipment—he and wife in matching
hand-knitted Swiss caps—got very high and mighty indeed. "Because he's my friend and a banker, that's why,"
he shot back, the boy being obviously vermin for having
opened his mouth at all. However, he seemed to think it
wiser to let those two go on and appropriate my place
instead. The mother had been on the side away from the
offender, with the machine hurtling the cars along too fast
for argument, but in the scene that ensued at the summit
she had plenty to say. A firebrand—one of those liberal
dames who never learned a decent respect for bankers and
may even respect the rights of ordinary citizens. That's
going pretty far but I'm sorry to say this rock-faced
middle-aged woman, perhaps driven to outrage more for
her child than herself, seemed to be somewhat of that
breed. Carried on as though unaware that the shabbiness

of her parka and old store-bought bonnet—not to mention skis three years out of fashion and bindings worse, transferred it was plain from a still older pair—made such behavior impermissible. Moreover she had quite a vocabulary at her command, nothing like the monotonous yowls, like handfuls of feces, same dull plop over and over, that we get from more up-to-date agitators.

A crowd was gathering, new arrivals off the gondola pausing to take in the show in spite of impatience after the long delay below, having paid $10 each to spend most of the day like that. (Line-watchers in force. Not many N.J. lawyer tricks successful on a Sunday like that.) The irate mother, as I came on the scene, was demanding the names of the culprits. Tykes as we'll call him, for tycoon genuine or phoney, flustered but well practiced in keeping a semblance of cool before outbursts from social inferiors, remarked on her lack of it—that old ploy, quelling an opponent through embarrassment over his head of steam. Better yet when relevant, get a flick in at his accent, i.e. by implication his lower-class if not immigrant origin. "My dear madam, your rudeness and extraordinary exhibition of ill-temper do you no credit and are absolutely unjustified, as I can easily sustain ..." with a pointed glance at her bindings followed by a casual one at his own. "My dear sir," said she, "if you think and you clearly do that the suavity of your diction excuses the boorishness of your behavior you are sadly mistaken." "I happen to be," he interrupted, warming up a little after all under the stares of the onlookers and growing nervousness of his wife and the moneybag couple, "a very old and useful friend to this corporation, I've done them many favors over the years, if I take what might look to you like a little advantage occasionally ..." "And I," retorted the lady, "and all my family have been for fifteen years members of the public without which this corporation could not exist. Not to mention the many friends who have skied here through us and whose resentment of such actions as yours is not commercially negligible." The wife and other couple were looking quite miserably at their ski-tips, not having been told to expect any such unpleasantness. "What's more, you're in a strange position to speak of rudeness. The way you spoke to my son down there would call for apology, even if you weren't being a thief as well." Now he's getting hot under the collar but still remembers the appropriate little laugh. "Such words, I must say ..." "Certainly. You stole skiing time, didn't you? from us and all these others."

He waved that off airily, though not yet quite daring to turn and beckon his companions to the start of the trail. "There was a wait of ten minutes. Do you really think that is worth making such a spectacle for? It was nothing, and as I say ..." At that her voice and stance became positively majestic with fury. Athena herself she had become, causing the banker et al. to dwindle perceptibly before her wrath, and oddly enough the boy standing in silence beside her, looking all this time neither participatory nor embarrassed for her but only very melancholy at some deep level of his being, also took on at that moment, from some slight lift of the head and light of anger in the eyes, a godlike beauty. "Ten minutes!" she shouted in her Olympian scorn. "It was fifty minutes. Liar! Cheat! We went through the line, not you, you sneaked in like rats at the head of it. We're the ones who can say how long it was."

Not one of the crowd so much as murmured, pro or con, although the theft had been from them too. No doubt they preferred to keep their resentment general— at "conditions," or fate—and perhaps some envied the dress and nerve of that elegant thug. She never got their names. A hard decision had to be made. Friends waiting, so much of the day shot already, so they gave up the notion I was sure they considered a moment, she and the boy, of going down behind the two couples and sticking to them the rest of the day if necessary—without a word more it would have been—until they drove them off the mountain and got their license number.

God forgive me, I've wished ever since that they had. In all the shuffles and shady deals there've been since then, receiverships, bankruptcy, creditors this and that, Tykes is certainly out of that corporate picture—if it was true he was ever in it. And of course I know what a fine specimen he is, how welcome at his clubs, how needed in the life of the nation. I just can't help wishing for the scene it would have been—the two couples who had thought to be Lords of the Mountain all day, immune to hoi polloi, getting more and more morose as the boy carves his swift, angelic semicircles every which way around and in front of them and behind too, where he'll appear as by miracle, to ridicule their more tentative tracks—they being the kind of undaring skiers with a lot too many private lessons written all over their impeccable style. In silence and with never a smile, certainly no suggestion of sneer, that's the way he would do it, I'm sure, even as he tightens the invisible net. Or nearly invisible, on that packed slope. On powder fields it would have been a stunning plumage and calligraphy.

The mother, not in his class by a long shot but of natural competence and good long experience, is never far behind, by dint of omitting his more fantastic whirligigs, and the portrait she too now presents is of nothing but concentration on the sport. Not even sidelong looks do the two of them cast at their prey, who try to elude them by speeding up on one steep pitch, a silly mistake which brings them some grief and humiliation—bruising them in their innate assumption of superiority as well as a flying limb or two—and then by protracted slowdown. No use. The enemy is not to be shaken off, nor will it be if they approach the gondola again as they did before and are so clearly entitled to, by the side door to the head of the line. To the disenchantment of his wife, and more consequentially of his friend the banker, who let's suppose was not that close a friend but just calculated to become one by the end of the day, Tykes is dreading another public showdown. Beneath him; too vulgar; they were just out for fun after all. Not for him to perish in the tumult, or lose another drop of sangfroid either. "Well, I guess we'd better call it a day." The pursuers note the license number as skis are hoisted to the rack. Then mother and son are enveloped in a white cloud and wafted instantly to the summit, via neither line nor lift. Kitty and David, as the other couple are undoubtedly named, sorely regret having accepted the invitation.

Just a modest scenario but I wish it had happened. However, I'm not sure Tykes didn't decide to call it a day anyway. Style and hat notwithstanding, he nearly fell on the only turn I saw him make, over a most commonplace mogul; his aplomb was a trifle undermined, perhaps his prospects too, after the assurances he must have given, the serene ease in arranging such matters that his tone alone would promise.

The chains of Loches. Come back to them. Important, in connection with my plight. Might have bearing on U.S. "business psychology" too—as if anything didn't.

Oh what a beautiful thing, this sunshine, and the Governor's helicopter nearly grazing our chimney (they say it's his) after the tempest. Air so sweet, it seems a holiday. Such a sparkle and freshness everywhere, of green here and blue above, you want to spend the day just breathing it. And the quiet! You could hear the faintest bird-squeak and snake-slither. Road caved in at several points in both directions, so we're marooned on what's become a quarter-mile atoll, in the "disaster area"—that term loved by all. Absence of vehicles awe-inspiring.

No power—that's all right; have the old outhouse; have kerosene and food for a while. The hurricane itself veered off somewhere. It was flood we got, worst since '38 they say and you can believe it. Days and days of rain and then the real thing, the hurricane-associated (correct term I trust) deluge, all day and all night, till the mountain could hold no more and burst at every seam with watercourses raging down upon us. What a turnabout and upheaval and marvel of suddenness. Like Pompeii, and just now earthquake in China, and all such. Dear old long-suffering Nature. Like a child meek and mild who lets his best toys be ruthlessly taken for hours and all of a sudden picks up the model boat, good heavy wood like true ships of old, no plastic job, and goes BANG! on the bad one's skull. Knocks him or her out cold.

Funny? Well usually no more than its counterpart drought they say—we hear tragic and millions of dollars, not in that order, dollars first—but also usually far away, so we shake our heads dolefully, without much genuine dole. Worse if a friend has a stroke, or we stub our very own toe. Sympathy's a word I don't cotton to; covers a multitude, never mind of what.

Interruption there. Pretty busy these last couple of days. Luckily the rowboat was right side up and not carried away so we had a boatful of rain water. No such thing as brook any more and couldn't go near the fury there in its place. Pond ruined. The torrent tore up and through it, depositing a ton or so of tree-trash and debris of every description. Two pumps ruined too but the two well-houses held, cover of one retrieved half a mile downstream. Exhilaration of this primordial kick in the teeth, from forces we go along thinking we have under our thumbs. Landscapes transformed; boulders roaring, crests sizzling, like all the lions of Africa with all the devils of hell poking them from behind, faster, faster! neighbors calling (phone not out for some reason) with stories to tell, help to offer if anybody could get here. Spirit of fresh racehorses wakened in the dullest souls—by the challenge for one thing: by God we can rise to it! and more by that benzedrine, humility. By God there are powers greater than we—what a fascinating discovery. The works of man, culverts 40 feet long and 6 to 8 in diameter, hurtling like drinking straws down the enormous chutes of the waters—now there's a pretty sight. Makes you giggle.

Quite a few houses too, we're told, toppled or swept

askew and in the nearest village, six miles away, a row still standing have a fifteen-foot drop at their front stoops, where the road used to be. Of course we couldn't get out to see that. A lot of underbrush can slowly straighten but acres of our lovely ferns, famous just here for size and variety, lie in swathes flat as bathmats wherever the water passed. No deaths reported, human that is, and beaver, mink, otter will get back to work; there must be corpses of other species around.

Then almost as suddenly it all subsided, leaving for a while the quickened sensibility, and the damage. Power back on. Roads partly patched. The machine monsters, trapped a day and a half, were let out ravenous and bellowing at last, one with proboscis waving fore and aft and appetite from treetops to bedrock indiscriminately. The mammoth rear of another flips like a toddler's pajama-bottom. Laboriously they smother the unseemly canyons, and like all counterrevolutions, nudge, scrape and shovel us back to the status quo. The birds are as alarmed by this racket as they were by the other; in any case they have made their new arrangements. The first day their dire losses had reduced them to sick, plaintive cheeps—all from ground level, under blueberry bushes or other unaccustomed and dripping shelter, all branches having become inimical. Our cat is out prowling again; so are their other enemies. The bears will be coming down soon for the little green apples, shaken prematurely from ramshackle trees planted a century or so ago when this was farmland.

The developers have had a setback. No chainsaws for three days now and their proud scars across the woods are still bogs. For the rest of us, this is not tragic. And another funny thing, recalling that tricky word sympathy. The only house nearby altogether toppled, upsydaisy, to smithereens, belonged to the one thoroughly dishonest, disagreeable and disliked woman in town. Had long since lost credit at the local store, for good reason, though reputed to have bank accounts here and there. Some say she's a witch, some that she makes her pile fabricating fake antique gravestones for sale to dealers. She had been evacuated, and is now railing at everyone, a little more than before.

Some lingering whiff of justice, all too rare we're told in these multi-million-dollar surprises, emanates from that. And if we smile at it, why, that only gives us still another bond with Noah, in our not having been washed absolutely pure after all.

Am I getting used to it? But I don't want to! Oh, I don't understand anything. So maybe *that's* what I don't want and am so brilliantly (?) dodging: understanding anything. Maybe I was lying back there, falling into that humdrum boast; how humiliating. People are always claiming they want to understand ("l'horreur de ne pas comprendre") but really when you think about it it's got to be a lie most often—one of those flattering self-delusions or run-of-the-mill masochism. No sense to it at all. What on earth would keep us going if we understood? Ergo, understanding or the attempt at it is the cardinal sin. Right? Imagine if an Olympic athlete tried to understand what he was doing—everybody'd think he was cracked, get the Valium, call the shrink. At the very least he'd fall and hurt himself. The thing is to *a*) enjoy the experience, and *b*) try to be better than somebody else, no matter what the sacrifice. (Bullock's entrails best, on appropriate altar.)

Sounds cynical and that I'm not, just somewhat shaky on my flippers these days, so there must be a flaw in the reasoning, if any reasoning has occurred. My old friend Bailey seems to have been wrong about my not needing philosophy, even though his didn't save him from apparently willful drowning, and my scant acquaintance with that haystack doesn't inspire me to look for the needle in it, even now in these, ouch, I was going to say *straits*—narrow body of water connecting etc. Put that needle in haystack in your pipe and smoke it. That's how bad it is. Wits wandering, confusion rampant, metaphors pounding at the gates, where only logic could prevail. Or religion—my goodness, high time I remembered that again; it plumb slipped my mind for several days, with the flood and all. Just when you'd think it would come to the fore, whereas in fact that's not the way it works. Shocks and excitements are raison d'être enough, or at least do away with the need of any. Only later you find that empty place. "Come Dio vuole," "the will of the gods"—how grand to be able to say that and really mean it. And idiotic? I think so; am not always so sure it matters whether it is or not. Depends a lot on weather and time of day and in that nice old saying, which side of the bed you got up on. If both sides wrong, no point to it, that must be why you never hear it any more.

Question, in short, of animal spirits. Èlan vital. How bizarre if that were the whole story. Well, it isn't, but I'm in no mood to play at discussing why. Weather unsettled again, wrong time of day, wrong side of bed. It's all so *serious.* Can't seem to get that through my head; or am not constituted for it. If so, tant mieux. A lot of good people have died laughing. Get back to business, to hell with imponderables, that's the American way: ours not to reason why, ours but to do and die ... Just one proposal though; just came to me; with proper packaging and PR work I bet it could be big, I mean really catch on. Get ready; hold your hats. It's the promotion of an attitude to be called Selective Comprehension—SelComp of course or some other heartwarming abbreviation pretty soon among devotees. Get the commentators to work on it first, with a subliminal reference here and there, as if it were something already established; then move on to college seminars in it, etc. same as they did with Thanatology. That's already faded out, there's a slot there, and this could be just the ticket. (Will clean up this prose before we get to merchandising.) What? you don't get it? Why it's clear as a Wheaties box. People are fed up, sick and tired, trying to act as if they had the answers to everything—life, death, Middle Eastern situation and so on. No, I didn't say trying to understand everything, nobody's that crazy; I said trying to *act as if.* Our little package will relieve them of that awful burden. You pick the part that suits you. If grief and death aren't your bag leave them alone, take something simpler—as many people do anyway but with some feeling of inadequacy or guilt. They'll be delighted to find they're in a regular movement, under such a dignified label, or perhaps we should say appellation.

For instance I know a woman who was truly, deeply stricken by her husband's death, until a militant friend took her in hand and explained to her that what had happened, far from a cause for sorrow, was a terrific stroke of luck, she could now *be herself* as never in the old regime, she hadn't known before how glorious it was to be a whole person, and so forth. So although the couple had had many pleasant times and years and several children together, and many tastes in common, she began telling everyone she was not only not upset but was *glad* her husband had "passed away" and she could have a few years to herself. She even became quite adept at saying so on public platforms. That's how liberated she got.

Some people might say the character that resulted had about the human density of a kid's balloon that got loose and drifted off over the zoo, until the gas fizzled out; if we can't grieve we are lightweight indeed, and all that sort of thing. The point is, there are plenty like her who can't grasp more than one or two aspects of life at a time —serially they may take in quite a few before it's over but not all at once, that's asking too much—and the movement I'm proposing would do wonders for their self-esteem. No, that's the wrong tack, come to think of it, for that case; the lady's self-esteem is doing fine, as it did in her previous configuration when she had no idea how deprived she was. But we can offer her a philosophical-sounding basis for what might otherwise appear a bit thin and shrill and in her case even treacherous. Details and strategy to be worked out; many other types of candidates to consider. Me for one; I don't seem to be getting hold of the whole too well either, that's why I thought of it. Sound trucks might seem cheap—we'll see; probably some sort of church trappings best, mixed with a few easy recipes from *The Joy of Psychoanalysis*. And of course a Leader but that's easy, we'll advertise for her in N.Y. Rev. of Bks. Dough's no worry, it'll come pouring out fast enough; give people a sense of community nowadays, they'll pay anything.

Storm gathered and slowly circling, again, all day—
a too heavy load of dirty sheets, some soiled nearly to
black, still going round and round, in a machine that keeps
promising breakdown or breakthrough every minute.
Patches of bright blue show now and then in the rips and
interstices, and brief shafts of Wagnerian sunlight that die
out with the next sluggish spin, as do the ominous spells
of wind, all sound and fury. Friend climatologist, sir, your
normalcy begins to offend. Just one day of honest to God
sun—o sole mio!—after the flood. Then a whopper,
though only an hour's worth, the first day the road was
in some manner passable: all Zeus's thunder and pitch-
forks of lightning along with another downpour. Visitors
arrived petrified, as much by the flimsy car-width fill-ins
along the road as by the rest of it. Candle in the window,
bottle on the bar, at such times show their true merit. So
another couple of good sociable friendly evenings—can
only speak for ourselves, of course; good talk, rather
hilarious round of charades ("aphrodisiacs," "ancillary"),
rousing four-hand comedy at the rattletrap upright piano
we got years ago for $25 (cost $100 though to get it here
and up the angled outside stairs). You'd think nothing
terrible was happening or had recently happened to anybody present.

Last night a bobcat was screaming bloody murder, just
up from the brook, I wonder what about. Like Achilles
when the river Scamander rises in wrath at his carnage
and takes off after him. Rivers are gods too, it's wise to
remember. And that one had had his fill of being clogged
with the corpses and stained with the blood of so many
Trojans even if Zeus had ordained it. Wonderful scene.

The time comes when a good river has had enough and cries No! you in your petty pride, strongest of men, I'll take no more of your slaughter, my banks are overflowing from it already; and great Achilles runs for dear life, stumbles, screeches like a bobcat at the injustice; after all, if Patroclus hadn't been killed he wouldn't ever have gone back to that battlefield, would have left the Greek ships to burn and gone back to a life of happy piracy (with twinges of guilt over the desertion, even if that fool Agamemnon had it coming to him?) and isn't loyalty to a friend high if not highest in the list of human motives? Scamander is being wicked, he feels—as we all feel toward some power or other when the tables turn, the jig is up. Ah, but there's a difference!—that's what makes your heart jump and your hair stand on end in that scene. It's not just the river speaking and rearing up out of its course. Achilles knows his doom; has known it all along. The trick is all in that. His mother Thetis knew it too, and so did Hephaestus the night he was forging that great shield. Achilles is prepared to be killed by Hector if he must be—since everybody knows how that match came out, and you can neither side with such a non-person as Hector even if you're pro-Trojan, nor warm to Achilles if you take him as a mere person, we can read that with equanimity—and only objects to being done in by a river instead.

He wants, in short, to be struck down by a proper antagonist. As who doesn't. Not by a mugger in the street, or a burglar in the house, or some sneak affliction from nobody knows where. But then there's a question of timing, that runs counter to the gist or tone of this treatise. It was also known to and accepted by Achilles that he would be killed in his prime, although his dangerous kind of life didn't make that by itself inevitable; Nestor and the other old ones had been fighting all their lives. But so, "by the will of the gods," it was to be. He must have been about the age of our noble friend Mike and the rat-girl Marcia. In these stories of ours, doom has gone bananas, is lumbering about like a headless monster; there's nothing to make us respect it. It is we, not Achilles, who must cry anguish by the brook or riverbank. And did I belittle shame a while ago? It's too easy for it to be sham, like sympathy, that's true, but the risk has to be taken. No choice. We've had our skiing time. It's when such as Mike are robbed of their ride that we have to weep.

Weep for Achilles, and Hector too, and far more for those cut down at the start without rhyme or reason.

But then do we give up the study, call it quits, let shame shut us up for the rest of our days? No; just try to keep a sense of proportion, that's all. Not that anybody can for long—if we had a decent one we'd all jump off a bridge. Just a stab at it now and then may be the only healthy way.

To recapitulate, as they say in academe: should I suffer less, or not at all, because others suffer more?

Yes. No. Yes. Maybe. Sometimes.

And if they suffer tremendously more, as many if not most do?

?

Actually I was thinking of lonely women taking to the bottle, and why so many doctors commit suicide.

But now look, a little old lady, with snow-white hair held up in a bun by old-fashioned hairpins, is coming down the path, twirling a stalk of fresh asparagus. She is nearsighted and bent way over, apparently looking for something between the flagstones. Why, it's my god-mother!—Maddy I call her, from the Italian *madrina*—and she's looking for the framed photograph of her dead husband, Joseph—Beppo to me, out of fondness and be-cause you don't call your elders by their first names. She's mixed up in her chronology, doesn't realize it's several years too soon for that, and the picture is by her bed in our guestroom; she never travels without it. "Here we are," I call. "We're planting zoysia grass, I'll be in to make tea in a minute," and as she slyly exhibits the stalk, "and oh yes, we'll pick a big bunch for dinner." In general her tastes are modest, in food as in everything, but asparagus is one thing she hankers for and never gets in the church home where she has lived the last few years, in Boston. "No hurry," she replies cheerily. "I'll read the children some more Matthew Arnold till you're ready." There too she is anticipating; the children are four and six. But she does know it is twelve and a half years since Joseph died, a gentle and learned man, to whom any roughness of speech or manner was unthinkable, and who never quite wrote a book. All the midnight oil he burned, and his pages of cramped delicate script from the thinnest of penpoints, had to do with minute notes on the works of Lope de Vega or far more obscure Spanish and Provençal poets. She was by nature an early sleeper and riser and as far as I know they never shared the same bed; otherwise, they had been, as the saying goes, inseparable. They had no children.

Having tried over and over and failed, because of her age, to get small jobs suitable to her breeding and intellect, as she has also failed to publish her literary efforts—memoir-type articles on their travels to China and elsewhere or some funny characters they had known, these last faintly fictionalized—she has calculated that their small savings can, with fearful frugality, be made to last her lifetime. Secretly she must know she is going to live too long, and it is panic that makes her jump ahead so, to the final years in one nursing home after another, when the few possessions she had left would slip away little by little together with her mind and bowel control and she would be sitting all day in her own filth, in a faded garment five sizes too big, taken from some fat stranger, dead or not quite.

The zoysia grass, bought on the say-so of a fine Madison Ave. florist, had arrived marked RUSH and PLANT AT ONCE! Children were parked out, engagements broken, work set aside. Backs aching, eyes blurring, hour after hour we disentangled the horrible little tufted needles from their wads—Hercules at his labors, Arachne at her web weren't a patch on us in our determination—and stuck them in the ornery soil, hundred after hundred, one by one, till time's wingèd chariot stopped hurrying near and passed us by altogether. The sun sank low, a crescent moon rose white, from the door my godmother called, "Are we going to have tea soon?" and an hour later, "Never mind, I've had my tea," and an hour after that, "Shall I start cooking the asparagus?" Alas, it was not even picked.

She is in a neat printed cotton dress, her own that time, a little long for the style of the year but she is handy with a needle and the mendings hardly show. We simply must not let her race ahead. She does it once as we eat our frozen peas, interrupting some quite witty remarks of her own on "Dover Beach" to look down and finger her sleeve in distaste, saying quite rudely, "Why did you put this on me? I never saw it before." "No, no, Maddy," I say with an affectionate pat on her dainty and always immaculate hand, to which her husband had penned a whimsical verse or two long ago. "That's not for a long time yet. Why, this isn't even the year when we try to get rid of the zoysia grass." Nevertheless she feels furtively at the back of her skirt and her glance goes hostile and wary as she eyes the door, watching for the head nurse, the one who will take her gold watch. At the end not even her engagement ring, a small sapphire to go with her fine blue eyes and tiny diamonds around, will be left, though she would never take it off. You'd think they'd have to cut her finger off to get it but the fingers were all there—maybe that's what she's checking on at the table now, holding her hand up to the light; perhaps it's with soap they manage, after her sleeping pill.

It becomes less of a leap. The years do pass, and although it is June again and she is wearing the same neat cotton dress, a little more mended, we are trying to get rid of the zoysia grass. Have already tried everything short of excavating the whole area to a depth of four feet and having it trucked away, so are doing that. Hideous, appalling vegetation. Cadmus-fashion, we might as well have sown a boxful of toenail parings and had them come up eels and octopuses, ugly green for two months and uglier brown for the rest. Our only happy days since that awful package came marked RUSH! had been when snow hid it all. Kills crabgrass, they say; I should think so —must kill a lot of horses too; it *is* crabgrass, only of such devilish strength and root system, no ordinary variety could exist near it. The stoutest coal miner's heart would quail at having to go down into that evil and tangled mass, of which the numberless members have each the muscle-power to strangle an oak. You can see moles and night-crawlers fleeing for their lives in all directions with the grass in hot pursuit. We told the Madison Ave. fellow we weren't asking for our money back, in fact we would gladly pay if he could only tell us how to get the stuff out of there, before it got to the house. He shrugged and said a lot of people were happy with it. People! happy! well, death-wish takes many forms, and there are many creatures moving among us disguised as people. So now we are watching the bulldozers at their mighty task and my godmother, asparagus in hand, is bent toward the flagstones, searching for something. I think that's the year the church told her she wasn't well enough to stay in the home any more—it was a residence for well-bred ambulatory ladies, not a nursing home—and she'd have to be out in two weeks. They must have meant her state of mind; she wasn't sick at all, had hardly ever been in her life, but she could be tactless and rather sharp-tongued when goaded, and a new woman put in as head administrator had gotten her goat. A terrible loss was the still older woman she'd made friends with there, a Scotch lady, who read Robert Burns aloud to her, now that her eyesight was failing. Besides, though my godmother knew pages of Burns by heart she loved hearing that authentic burr to it. It made her laugh—"Wee, sleekit, cow'rin', tim'rous beastie" and other such. She had a very merry laugh, like a schoolgirl's they used to say when teen-agers still laughed in her innocent kind of way, and all sorts of things still brought it ringing out at that time.

But she is also saying "I think I have to go home now," when she has just unpacked her cheap little brown cardboard suitcase held shut with fiber straps, and put her bottle of mineral oil in the bathroom and her hairbrush, with which she does a hundred strokes a day, on the dresser. She uses blueing too, having maintained a certain vanity about that once-blond superfine hair that turned white at thirty and still adds up to a thick braid at night. By home to get back to she means whichever place in the series it is, hard bed or soft, dark room or sunny, where all the time she lived for the coming visit with us. They have frightened her; she is in terror of breaking a rule or a dish, spilling something from her tray, having one of the attendants angry at her. Also she has left some things wherever it is and knows they may not stay where they belong overnight. We tell her the machines have finished, it will be quiet tomorrow, and the zoysia grass is not really dangerous, besides it has all been taken away. That's a lie, to this day it is still coming up, but we have to comfort both her and ourselves. We say the children have been begging for her to come and read Matthew Arnold to them. We eat pounds of asparagus, and laugh over verses of Beppo's that she and I remember, and funny sights we've seen together, like the street full of elephants under our window one morning in Rome. The picture is by her bed. Sometimes we speak of his funeral; there are certain things about that that she can laugh at too.

It was raining cats and dogs, on the little country cemetery that she herself had seen only once years before, when they visited the grave of his parents. Maddy and Beppo had never lived anywhere near it so it was not exactly a homecoming, but all his teaching had been in ugly cities that they never felt much at home in either, so this had been planned long before as more of a connection, as well as a great deal more charming. That was a word they both frequently used and an attribute they sought out, in Chinese prints and Sicilian donkey-carts as in minor Spanish sonnets. "Blow, winds, and crack your cheeks," a ruined king howling at the elements "from his little world of man," was never their style. Royalty and ruin alike had no bearing on the picture of life they so fondly shared. Yet it did rain cruelly that day in Massachusetts, in the village where his aged Aunt Tillie alone, of his relatives, still lived. In fact she was the only living relative in general of either of them. Not a niece or nephew existed, except possibly some bastard offspring of her older brother who had lived on nobody knew what and died, no less secretively, in France; her younger brother, "unbalanced" as they said in those days (meaning "disturbed," he "had problems") came to grief early, and Beppo had been an only child. So it was from Aunt Tillie's charming and choice and big colonial house on the green that we set forth, in a rattletrap hired conveyance provided by the undertaker and which showed very plainly what he thought of our little party. It needn't have been so little. The principals (the departed and the bereaved) were well liked and sociable, with a network of dear and lifelong friends and a readiness to make new ones, so if this had been in their last university town or anyplace accessible there'd have been a fair turnout. As it was, a couple of younger ex-colleagues or ex-students now working nearby had made it, and a junior bank officer in charge of their paltry finances, plus the two black-suited pros hardly bothering to keep on their mourning masks—maybe a dozen in all. The minister would meet us at the cemetery.

Aunt Tillie however was delighted, hadn't had so many guests or perhaps any in ages, and although she hadn't thought to provide refreshments or a clean guest towel in the bathroom, she flounced arthritically about with glittering eyes, nearly smashing all manner of heirlooms in her impatience to point them out with her cane, and crashing through various sad remarks with a series of stentorian and irrelevant yells, being close to totally deaf and averse to admitting it through the use of a hearing aid. The quite valuable antiques (early New England highboy, French Empire desk etc.), bric-a-brac once treasured in association with now long since forgotten travels, and fill-in pieces due for the Salvation Army, made just such a combination as always figured in the far more humble, rented apartments Maddy and Beppo had lived in; his professor's salary was below peak to the end and they never did have a house of their own. Publish or perish! so perish he did, of cancer, at sixty-three.

Aunt Tillie refused an arm or any assistance from the ghouls, not that she was aware of their status; she kept addressing them as Professor What's-your-name-again. She clapped a black straw frying-pan onto her topknot and brandishing a Japanese paper parasol to express her opinion of the pelting rain, scampered out and into the back seat of the vehicle; car you could hardly call it, though it did convey us over several miles of mud with only one flat tire and a sporadically choked gas-line. "Well, isn't this nice!" she bellowed as it coughed into a semblance of motion. "A real family gathering. Though I don't know who *you* are," she said jabbing me with an elbow. "But never mind, I suppose I should know. Just like old times." Half a mile on she shrieked, "But where's Joseph? Haven't seen him in years, don't know if I'd even recognize him, he's probably changed so. They say we all do. Wasn't he supposed to be here?" Maddy, on the front seat beside the driver, pointed to the urn on the floor by her feet. "Here." "What?" She pointed again. "Oh. Burned up, eh? I hope they don't do that to *me*. I like the old way best."

Another fit of curiosity seized her at the grave, among the umbrellas which various people kept trying to hold over her. As the minister was starting she decided to examine the hole and nearly slipped in. "Doesn't look very deep," she commented, as we yanked her from the brink. "It's hard to get good workmen for anything these days." The minister began again. "And who are those people?" she yelled at him, pointing at the double stone alongside. His father and mother, somebody managed to tell her, and with extreme gestures calling for hush, pointing to lips, prayer book and fresh-dug earth like the beginners' class in mime school, we were able to get our heads bowed and the words intoned. She said goodbye to nobody afterwards, scampering lopsidedly to her door, frying-pan and parasol flapping, as if the whole thing had been a terrible imposition and probably a case of mistaken identity as well. Maddy and I joined the jr. banker and ex-colleagues for a sandwich somewhere by the road. On the stone that was finally erected Maddy had her name and birthdate engraved too, to save trouble for whoever there might be to take it, never imagining it could be twenty-four years before that second date would be inscribed. It was a sunny fall day and there were far fewer of us that time, only the new minister and a Korean student who was visiting him, and the two of us fresh from another round with a bulldozer against the zoysia grass. At least there was none of that to disturb Aunt Tillie's bones, which must have been somewhere near. It was very short. We slipped the minister a check, with smiles and thanks, took a snapshot of the grave, laid down our bouquet and wiping away a few tears went on our way.

The savings had been used up some months earlier, and the picture vanished well before that—taken I suppose for the Italian leather frame, faded and frayed though it was—but she was spared knowing either of those developments, or that her fine white hair had been cut short, no doubt for sale, under pretext of treating the skin infection that had reached her scalp. Anyway by then the hair had been allowed to turn a dingy yellow straggling across her face, held up if at all by cheap little pins nothing like her own—fifty to a wad no bigger than a pack of chewing gum. That must have been in about the seventh or eighth place, an elegant one in appearance, adapted from a country mansion where I had once been to a debutante dance. When I first asked where the photograph was she said rather crossly, "Beppo? Joseph? Who are they? I never knew anybody by those names."

So she bends over searching as she comes down the path. Not for her girlhood which was made miserable by an ailing mother and a father of violent moods; she never had dared ask a friend home and never later wanted any part of it in recollection. Shadow before and after. The thirty years of marriage were all her light, if passionless no matter and that can't be known; when two are of such a feather, a mate sharing the perch can be bliss and miracle enough. Sometimes she picks up an actual feather from the ground and eyes it as if it were a jotting in some stranger's handwriting, which would tell her the secret if she could decipher it, even though the question will not be fully put for some years to come. She lets the feather fall and summoned as by a schoolbell hurries in to her reading; she must store up all she can while vision lasts, not that anybody has yet said it will not. There too, in the books as between the flagstones, she looks for the face and the gentle voice that belonged with it, which even before they were stolen the first time, in the flesh, had not really told her where to look for whatever it is. But then, dear Beppo, why should you have? Then there was no need, even if you did love to dance and she would grieve you at balls with her woodenness and refusal to smile at inanities. She made up to you in plenty for that, and then took the hard part on her own shoulders for twenty-four years.

Or perhaps it's a smaller thing she wants to find, small as the sapphire an impoverished suitor, by correcting a thousand extra student papers, would buy for his beloved, while the curved moon comes up white and the asparagus goes to seed and another seed, of wrack and ruin, goes in the ground with each nearly invisible sprig of zoysia grass. If only she could find it, whatever it is, she would be satisfied and stop making the worst happen now, and now, and now, until at last it's not ahead of time any more.

Friends of all ages for the weekend. Long struggle to clear flood damage from pool in time—partly successful, water still muddy but swimmable and temperature delicious; sun and first real heat of the summer; tennis—in which this new incompetence riles but I pretend not or not too much and whack away cheerfully, not keeping score any more, in secret bouts with whatever charitable companion may be around, when the court I love so would be otherwise unused. How beautiful it is up there in our still woods, especially toward late afternoon when the sun strikes only on the snow-white double birch at the NE corner; we were so lucky not to lose that in the clearing, or the great pine at another corner and the still grander one, P.'s tree-house still in it at awesome height, beside the bug-house. Of course the birds are not singing much any more. Early in the summer when the sun was low a pair of thrushes who live up there by the court were giving out their virtuoso stuff, more viola than winds I'd say, though an oboe might be invented subtle enough for it, undeterred by bang of balls or curses at shots missed or even the occasional yawping motorbikes of the juvenile set, from a vacation home or "secondary residence" five miles around the mountain. Yes, all right, our place could be called that too and no doubt is by others, and no doubt it's smug to think at least we're not destroying what's left of peace and wilderness with those earsplitting imbecile machines, snowmobiles either. Ugly words too, *secondary* and *vacation*. What can they mean?

Charmed days, all of these. Charmed summer altogether, a bolt of precious silk shaken out sky-high, all ripples of many-colored happiness. Get back on the job, elf. The theme is affliction. OK, it's not forgotten. But meanwhile, as usual after guests and all those bunks slept in, I've hung a lineful of sheets etc. and among the hues of that fancier fabric—see above—the white is more fascinating than all the flags of the U.N. More useful too but I'm speaking of what's to be rejoiced over. Brook and sunset restored, and old Priam has made his stupendous visit to Achilles in his tent by the ships, to beg for Hector's body so that he may be properly mourned and sent off by fire, not eaten by dogs and kites. Scene of awful sorrow and worse coming after the last page—the twelfth day dawning, when the battle for Troy will resume—but rejoice we do at there being paper with such words on it, and here in our small enclave at the reading aloud, new bond and pleasure all these weeks. We all know it, not forgetting it's the booby prize brought on by my trouble, but just the same as splendid as all Priam's gifts to the killer of his son.

A fortuitous aspect of the same prize is our being here all four together, first whole summer in years—P. and E. thank God for their own reasons, not because Ma's in distress; I would hate that, as they know. No, it just happened to happen and they too, soon to be off again, speak in some discovery of how good it feels to be a family. They have gotten at times rather fed up being only with their—oh dear—"peers," people their own age, all with more or less the same run of problems, and are glad of a mixture of ages for a change, though their friends who come to visit are bright, busy, good company every one —no Marcias nor any shadow of one—and a lot more help at kitchen and other chores than one batch of ours a while ago. Rash in that one case to ask them. We had only known them at dinner parties, a most undependable method of acquaintance. Still, all agreeable in other ways. But what a pesky little weekend legacy, that resentment you try to squash and dislike yourself for, at Gloria's not having lifted a finger (there's one cliché worth preserving, states the case quite well; too bad "lift a leg" means against fire hydrant) while you and your daughter, she moreover sick with a summerlong virus, get the meal together and on and off the table and the things scrubbed that don't go in the dishwasher and the machine in due course emptied and things put away etc., and Paul and Stanton or Fred and Spike or Peg and Meg ditto, leaving glasses and ashtrays on the porch for you to bring in and not thinking of sweeping still less rolling the tennis court, not so the thought fathered the deed anyway, though they were the ones using it most of the time. Degrading, this feeling; to your knees, host and hostess, smear your faces with dirt. Very rare though in our experience, in our house or anybody else's—something to be said for the egalitarian (?) society, or perhaps as my lawyer companion of the ski-lift put it, we don't move in the right circles.

Anyhow, nothing of the kind from any under-thirties for some years, in fact it was two just out of college who saved the Argive ships that time, quietly appearing in the fray whenever help was needed, armed with potato-peeler etc. or just willing hands and feet and the wit to use them most effectively, with never a "Let me know if there's something I can do" from behind newspaper on sofa across room. Twin Hermai in disguise they were, sent in a kindly mood by the Lord of Thunder to veil the failings of other members of the party and keep spirits high for the duration. Far from those two noble heads was any thought of free-loading, such as we'll see in Odysseus' house. But that comes later. And the weekend in question comes earlier; before the flood; before I developed this trick of keeping out from underfoot, hereafter to be referred to as KOFU. Could that be the reason for the unbecoming resentment? Painful but to be considered. Perhaps they lifted finger, leg and all as much as the noble youths, carried glasses, rolled court, and I—at loose ends, time on my hands, thoughts in turmoil, sorry for myself and craving grievance—made up the other picture out of whole cloth. Hideous possibility; that way lies the septic tank and yourself flushed into it. But honestly I think not —not yet. I clearly remember Ennie and me being over the sink and out of the high-toned conversation to an

unusual degree that weekend and her virus thriving on it
so she was back in bed for three days, and rolling the
court myself on Monday because Prodge, always splendid in such matters, was in a boat-building crisis and had
to drive to Boston for a tub of resin. Also remember
washing the dust, or was it ashes, from my face. That
clears the air. What a reprieve.

Nobility—angry word—how dare we use it now? It
brings us Mike F., that last visit, a year ago, not in any
knowledge of his doom. No way for that to be, but what
happened is not to be believed either. Why, he was a mick,
a comic, a story-teller, of small build too and wearing
thick glasses, no Achilles whatsoever, no reason for fate
to be after him so soon. E., to whom he'd been the best
of several extra, non-blood brothers, for a long time
couldn't speak of him without tears. He was with us for
a few days, with the baby daughter, fourteen months old,
who lived with him about half the time—sad arrangement
and I couldn't see how he managed with all the legal-aid
work he'd taken on aside from making a part-time living
in a law office. They had the same laughter and out on the
grass in the sun would be mimicking heroes and villains
ranging from Cuchulain to Babe Ruth and the Teamsters'
Union which he'd been engaged in some risky hassle with.
He had a pack of friends his own age but no peer-worship
—matter of fact I don't know anybody worth his salt
who has, some psychiatrist must have made it up. For
Mike, anyway, we were all in the same kit and caboodle
and if he had favorites he wasn't playing them—"Caboodle," said the baby, with exactly his owlish solemnity
before the punch-line. "Poppa, more caboodle!" And they
grinned at one another. He too wielded scraper, scouring-
pad, pool-skimmer, remembered the dog's milkbone, ran

for the missing glass, gave thought to canvas or MS for whoever wanted to show such wares, rattled off his wry tales of gangster weddings and County Kerry forebears out of the pub only when necessary to avoid the clink.

Much later we began to know to what lengths he'd gone in goodness to other people. Time, money, sympathy—he'd lend or give extravagantly, but with a grain of hard sense to it always—no sucker for phoneys; shucked off Joe the Hippie and his girlfriend from Outer Space pretty fast. I'll get around to that pair if I keep feeling like it. They're the ones who worked the G. family for all they were worth at the apartment they rented down in the village here one winter. Mike could say no thanks to that kind and their blabber of love—as he relayed it, "Gotta love everybody, gotta love yourself first of all, even when you're fucking up"—but knocked himself out for plenty of others. That could be, it makes sense now, why a wife with the ambitions that one had would leave him, but not why the river Scamander ran after him. He had bloodied no streams, offended no gods seriously. It was not time for his doom, would never have been the time for that one.

The mugger was sixteen, convicted of another murder a year before, out on weekend parole. Very poor family; low IQ, low everything; a nobody; the kind Mike had been working for.

By one of the stranger chances in our Homer-times, it was his friend and ours, in age midway between—architect, Jewish, call him Jake, close to Mike's double in comic twist of mind—whose turn to read the other night fell on the absurd Olympic-type games bossed by Achilles, ending the funeral rites for Patroclus. Comic relief though not originally and serving a deep enough

purpose, after the strains of war and mourning and with
the heart-racking immensity of Priam's visit about to follow. A lot of common sense there; we relax, so do the
Greeks, in the luxury of everyday angers and vanities.
How dare you cheat an older man and son of Atreus in
the chariot race, you whippersnapper, or you, Odysseus,
kicking the knees of far stronger Ajax out from under
him in the wrestling match. First prize one mule, second
prize one woman. He read it a mile a minute, the born
sports announcer, making it a little funnier than it should
be, all home runs and fixes, though he read the words on
the page. Life, the show, must go on; it would be wrong
to mourn forever. It was just the way Mike would have
read it.

He had no father alive to play Priam for him; the old
king's gifts in any case served only ritual, though crucial
for proper entry into the world of death, and could not
have forestalled death. That had to come. Athena's dirty-
work (makes it hard being on her side later but can't be
helped, that's the way the chips fall) only hastens it—
making Hector think he has a brother fighting beside him,
so that he stops his dreamlike running, running, three
times and more around the walls of Troy with huge
Achilles resplendent in god-forged armor after him, and
turns at last to fight. And the victor's own doom is not far
off. He knows it; knows too that human life is short at
best, honor is all and misfortune not to be argued with.

Oh but this worse dream occurs, over and over in all
our heads, by other walls than Troy's, and nothing to run
from even until it's all over—too late. Jake's wife Ruth
was suddenly beating the banister as we said goodnight
and the tears came at last, fast, bitter. "Oh damn, oh God
damn!" Mike had brought them groceries and helped

clean house for a month one time when she was flat with a ruptured disc, and drove their three small children to grandparents in Indiana so Jake could stay with her for the operation.

It was a week before *it* happened that he went his way, with the loving oversized smile that you couldn't by any stretch call handsome though it made the laundry brighter on the line, in his decrepit old Plymouth he said he'd tried to bribe a friend not to give him, the baby a little sunburst of kisses, goodbyes and general rapture in the strap-seat beside him. We were to meet again soon.

The pool is nearly clear; the beautiful boat-under-construction has been turned on its side today—a celebration! Two other young friends have come; older ones tomorrow. Weather sparkling, marvelous—thanks for that, with all my heart. I'll whack at tennis balls, or at where they seem to be from the sound of the first bounce.

Charmed days. Scary ones. I dread the leaves turning. Hated coming to the last line of the book. "So they performed the funeral rites of Hector, tamer of horses." But now we'll start the Odyssey and see how far we get.

I find I mind the new clumsiness, and even the humiliating fear of hurting oneself—by burning, cutting, stumbling—quite a lot less than the new kinds of ignorance, being cut off from so many sources of fact and opinion one was scarcely aware of being nourished by, it was so natural to have them. Magazines for one. All sorts, even silly or in other ways annoying; they keep your wits working. I can foresee becoming a *mental* cripple and already have fallen into sneaky little ways of covering up for not being on the ball, not having kept up, having missed this and that. It goes in geometric progression. You lose interest, then will I suppose, then capacity. My god-mother became sly that way toward the end. I would say, "Would you like me to bring your supper tray out here on the terrace?"—this in one of the rest homes or what-ever they call them when she was no longer able to visit anyone—and she would say with a canny gleam, "What would *you* like?" although of course I wouldn't be eating there. It was just to conceal that she didn't quite know where she was and whether it was supper or breakfast time or whether a tray on the terrace was possible or permissible. Or if a meal was in order at all; perhaps she had already had it, or was supposed never to eat again. She wouldn't have minded any of the possibilities, especially the last, only hated being caught in a stupidity. I under-stand.

Yet in the beginning, the aspect most like some form of insanity—or so I imagine—almost made me laugh. It was interesting. I think I'd have laughed if it hadn't been for the slight nausea it produced. Cars zooming down at you from the sky or up from out of the ground, a highway seen from a train window turned to a roller-coaster better than anything in Coney Island, no straight line anywhere, doors and windows wiggling, columns teetering each at a different angle—perilous but funny, quite a new con-ception in architecture; and every face a grotesque. Your own dear husband bends to kiss you with a huge crooked mouth coming out of his ear and two noses or none. Naturally you laugh, and hurt his feelings. But that was the "active" phase, only a few weeks; lines are straight again; now we're down to (I can't resist it, horror in language has its own charm) the nitty-gritty. No, I take that back, there are limits even to horror, I mean in its power to charm. That one's just plain atrocity. Make it brass tacks or that old stand-by reality, dull but honest and reliable, or anything you like. Whatever we're down to, the comedy has gone out of it. For laughs will have to look elsewhere, try harder.

Not that I think insanity is funny. That's too outdated, went out with race and Polish jokes except in the worst sixth-grade set. We're a humane society, big-hearted; we care about the afflicted, unfortunate, unlucky—ethnically, economically, physically; unless we're murdering them in the street for fifty cents or opposing (or vetoing) bills in Congress that might give them a leg up, or if it's legless they are, something to sit on. You can't expect our heroes of commerce, or their lobbyists and other myrmidons, to indulge their big hearts at the expense of the national economy. Off the ski-lift with them, if they were so frail. Also we can't spread our sympathies too thin and it's so easy to make a mistake. Do you side with the octogenarian cripple who was stabbed or his/her fifteen-year-old killer, out after his/her third offense of the kind? And of that death that must keep occurring for the rest of our lives, in all of us who were close? "These kids have rights too," said the manager of the correctional facility from which Mike's murderer—and for his little daughter something worse—was out on parole. Why of course. So you deplore the whole business and nobody can deplore more than a few minutes a day. The show must go on. There are bigger things, like Energy, not the human kind, to think of.

But Bedlam, not the figurative kind, it's not considered decent to consider it funny any more. You can't even deplore it, it's too complicated, better left to specialists, though if you can spare a soft spot you might object to some instance or other of overcrowding or brutality or even medical incompetence, on which last you're probably just guessing. Anyway it's wise to suspect yourself first. Too many of us just have to be *agin* something; we know what to think of that type of temperament.

No, I wasn't being light-hearted about that most awful of sufferings, as I suppose it must often be. The whacky world I saw for a while was funny because of a whale of a difference from the real thing, at least I hope so—hope there's a difference, hope that's why it was funny. Probably nobody knows when they're crazy so it's hard to be sure. Anyhow I never thought the cars were flying out of the air or the ground, or buildings being made to topple, with the sole intent of injuring *me*, or with any reference to me whatever. It was perfectly clear to me, roller-coaster and all, that they didn't even know I existed, just like a lot of doctors and nurses (not speaking of recent encounters, all kind and good as I've said). So, having known quite a few people who do think planes are being sent to buzz them or the TV set in the hospital room is being repaired at 6 A.M. out of specific animosity, I gathered I was sane and could laugh, through my tears, at the odd aspect of things. The tears weren't all that frequent either; let's not exaggerate.

That next phase, though, of time-killing, that might be more borderline. On this subject the Iliad's no help, none I can think of at the moment. *Dead Souls* is better—have been hearing installments of that too. 19th C. Russia in general has a good deal to offer in that department, only unfortunately the characters you could learn from are usually rich and suffering from the explicit disease of boredom. They go on and on about it; it's the next-to-prime topic, after Mother Russia herself. Kinetic and middle-class as we are, even the most truly bored among us would no more think of putting it that way than of discussing Mother America. No other nation I know of has gone in for it as a general trait, which might mean the Russians of that time were the only honest people on earth, and 1917 destroyed a national treasure of candor. French *ennui* only gets full treatment through reaction to it (*A Rebours*). André Gide said he wrote "pour me désennuyer le matin"—as I am learning to do, in distinction from other impulses with the same result. In other words boredom didn't suit him, he took measures against it, would not have liked to be known à la russe as The Man Who Was Bored. No Frenchman in his right mind would. Only pre-Lenin Russians made it a regular category in the human laundry list, and if I'm not mistaken it was only a male type at that. Loads of women were undoubtedly just as bored but didn't go around saying so; it wasn't their generally accepted designation.

I suppose the Greeks camped out there by the beach year after year must have gotten pretty bored too between battles and that's why Agamemnon got so petty and brought on all the rumpus with Achilles, without which there'd be no story. That's not the explanation he gives himself when he gets around to apologizing; he says the Lord Zeus addled his wits, or as we would say, society was to blame. Personal responsibility for one's actions was not a popular notion even then; it's not designed to be; it takes a twisted mind to really go for it. Whatever Agamemnon said, it's plain he had been bored a day too long, and if the Commander-in-Chief was, think of the common soldier. But that was just a single if protracted expedition, not a way of life. Doesn't tell you anything about killing time as a serious art, and not much about how it was done even in a particular circumstance. Play gin rummy, gas on the telephone, hang around outside the drugstore, gape at TV or not gape just sit in front of it . . . There are ways and ways, and I've perhaps been confusing time-killing with boredom—easy to do when one's a newborn babe at both. But of course they're not the same thing at all, in fact those months when I applied myself to that discipline —I called it art but I suppose it's a social science—I admit I did get bored, through lack of skill. Not so the couple warming themselves in the ski lodge one sub-zero afternoon.

Season-pass people but not from nearby, far from it. An amiable chatty pair with a son of eleven and middle-bracket equipment, not the kind who hog space by the fire or bump boiling coffee over your hand, make trails a menace and any lodge an inferno. That brutish arrogance, sad by-blow of mass democracy, had taken so little in their case they weren't even critical of it—the worst thugs in these amusement situations, as we social scientists call them, being always the quickest in outrage at anybody else who behaves as they do. Every weekend all winter the easy-natured family drive twelve hours from and back to New Jersey, like millions of others from whatever home base they need that desperately to flee— Long Island, Rhode Island, Mass. for less roadtime, Delaware a lot more—ostensibly for about eight hours at a sport they may be no great shakes at (weren't in this instance) but really more for reasons you could call both simpler and more devious. That's not counting this rather hyperactive version of the singles syndrome—a pretty strenuous way to make acquaintances, but the hunger is that pervasive; some of the buses are even from Wisconsin

and Minnesota, those too getting back in time for work
Monday morning though not with the same clientele
quite every week.

The woman and I were more or less in each other's laps
by the fire and she had just helped me mop up the coffee
from my parka and given suggestions for the burn. "But
I should think," I said, "that you'd have to spend all the
rest of the week getting over one weekend and getting
ready for the next one." "We do!" A sudden smile illu-
mined her face, as if I'd hit on the happiest aspect of the
marriage and a very happy one indeed, redolent of many
sorts of contentment. The husband, an electrician I think,
of Scandinavian cast, also nodded in beaming confirma-
tion. "There's all the laundry and the food things to put
away and wash up and the mess in the car"—she made it
sound more and more gratifying—"and usually there's a
tire or a ski-edge or zipper or something to get fixed. And
by then it's Thursday"—the word Thursday brought a
new glow of delight to both their faces—"and I have to
market and get some cooking done ahead for the weekend, because everything has to be packed and ready before we go to work Friday, except a few last-minute
freezer things . . ." She ended on a little note of triumph,
well aware that a less modest one would have been justified. "And here we are!" We expatiated together on times
of abominable road or skiing conditions, mountain all ice
as it nearly was that day, fatal pile-ups and highways
closed from blizzards, etc. none of which had yet kept
them from their appointed round, and then the husband
summed up with an insight little short of majestic, though
keeping the smile and commonplace tone of voice befit-
ting the occasion. He said—how could one ever forget it?
—"It makes the winter go faster."

Oh yes indeed it must! and the goal is but the grave.
Not an uncommon view of it, but no ordinary mortal's
lips uttered the brilliant capsule of words. That had to be
some god or goddess in disguise, perhaps the grey-eyed
one herself, speaking for two seconds across the rude
steaming scene, among the thick-padded gloves spread
out to thaw and noses and toes being massaged back to
sentience, and over the nearby male voice not so much
raised in anger as chronically raised and angry, emitting
over and over the same two despairing yawps, "I yaw-
reddy toledja!" and "Doan gimme that!"

Art, discipline, science my foot. What I had been hearing about was time-killing of such expertise only the
deepest innate wisdom could account for it, and try as I
might to emulate it in my months of effort, I had to admit
failure. I'm shallow; just wasn't born with the gift. For
one thing, as I said, I got bored and the couple in the ski
lodge plainly prove that that shows inferior technique,
and probably a lack of basic commitment. To be first-rate
at anything you have to stake your all. Nobody's an artist
"on the side." From fine or at least runaway novelist to PR
desk and in short order, that's the way it goes when true
heart and/or talent aren't there, and the way it went for
me in my brave new undertaking. At killing time I was
a fake but it took a lot of hard work to make me realize
it. I strained the budget with phone bills, called people I
hadn't thought about in years, talked to closer friends half
an hour instead of three minutes; thought up dinners that
would take hours to prepare, whether with any benefit in
taste experience or not; tried on ten dresses in a shop
instead of two; vacuumed room after room without let or
mercy—"How nice your house looks!" people exclaimed
to my dismay or worse; a dull rage filled me at these kind

remarks, about the quiches and the boysenberry tarts and crêpes Geneviève too. I wanted to bash such friends' faces in with a skillet or vacuum the hair off their heads—not that some didn't have worse troubles of their own. One becomes unfair, another form of derangement.

The difficulty, I saw at last, was in not having a blue-print. If you're going to kill time, without either habit or natural talent to direct you, you must lay out its shape very precisely, not let it straggle all over the place so you're giving it a whack here or a bite or a kick there without serious results; next thing you know it's spread-ing out before you with as many hours a day as ever. Retired people, used to office or some other regular regime, are said to have this trouble. But I was in the same location, never had had to take trains to work, hadn't for years had a boss or been one; nothing was changed except everything. I never had thought of an occupation as a raison d'être or imagined the abyss of not having one either, only vaguely pitied certain friends of various ages who never latched on to a métier, or the one, dear charm-ing C. B., at sixty still the promising young one, who contrived with agonizing slowness and evasion of the truth to give his up for the fleshpots. He learned to kill time all right but not happily, not like my acquaintances in the ski lodge. They were the ones to take as a model; only with that serenity could it really work. So I made a chart, just mentally but still a careful one, of minutes, seasons and the rest of it, but every night some ghost of my old self must have been down in the great hall unravel-ing it, to keep the suitors at bay—as if the lifelong tricks of the trade might one day by miracle return.

It will pass, our Christian Scientist friends said a while ago; it's only temporary, and we spoke no more of it, can't think how it happened to get mentioned at all. You don't discuss venom with snake-handlers or statistics with sociologists or structure with structuralists. From each according to his need and more power to them all. If it's Error they'd have me in I couldn't agree more, only on specific causes and effects I can't get around to envying their certainties. Doubt remains a luxury I won't do without.

Time wouldn't stay on my chart, kept crawling off the edges and all over. I gave up and for a while drifted disconsolately, without even that incentive.

He was short but huge-torsoed and strong as a forklift, with a light brown beard that didn't exactly get to flow but was all over the place, mingled at spots with another tangle that must have started from his scalp. I really can't keep up much interest in this fellow, Joe the Hippie, except for what I'm about to tell you. Still, all those other fine crooks got mentioned so this love-everybody variety might as well be too. And he wasn't without talents; knew a good deal about repairing antique furniture and could whistle a lot of Beethoven and even Mahler themes, had a vast collection of tapes and records. He'd done a little time in a third-rate college and was odd-jobbing when we first knew him, helping a somewhat bigger-shot dropout, that is with his ALS a little sturdier for the moment, on a small carpentry job for us. They got the leaning cobblestone chimney of the cabin leaning the other way and put in some plumbing that quickly froze —they forgot the outlet or something. Don't tell me hippie is a dead-duck word. I only call him that because our friend Harry down the road, who's not partial to beards, always did and everybody around got in the habit. Cooking tiger-lily blossoms was one lesson we got from Joe.

He had a way of latching on to our guests while on that job and it paid off with the G. family. Not that they're fools, any more than Mike was, but Joe went easy on the corn in the beginning, talked music quite sensibly and did good work fixing their rocking-chairs, so when they went to Europe for three months they let him stay in a little barn apartment the boss-dropout had fixed up and the G.'s rented for ski-time. No rent, from Joe; he was just to do some insulating that had been left undone and take care of the G. cat. It was an old and much-loved marmalade, they even left cat-food for the whole time, and came back to a misery, not only on that front. Apparently the Calo and Friskies had been turned in—not at the local store but farther away—against soybeans etc. The cat was eventually found nearly starved in a cellar miles away, the insulation was still missing and Joe, as the family arrived, was moving with girlfriend into a barracks room adjoining the apartment. The owner had said he could and the G.'s had no claim on that part of the upstairs, so all right.

She's the one from Outer Space, calls herself Andromeda, or maybe Andromache which makes no sense but that wouldn't be a deterrent. "Love love love," they sang, they crooned, they lectured, they excoriated. She had fine long brown silky hair and would slip behind it with a smile of deep mystery when asked about her astronomical origin. Turned out she was also in the process of inheriting half of Arizona but the G.'s didn't know that when the grocery bill began getting so big. For a while they blamed themselves for extravagance. When they caught on, they got a blast from a side of Joe quite new

to them. "You and your rich bourgeois friends! and your
petty little accountant psychology! I don't see how you
stand your own stink. Like can you give me one good
reason why plodding, obtuse, workhorse types like you
shouldn't buy a few groceries for superior spirits the
whole hope of the world lies in . . ." Honestly. As the male
G.'s are much bigger and not far behind him in muscle
and chest expansion, and Poppa doesn't take too much
pushing around, I imagine his wife had to make some
calming signals. And the girlfriend did her little drifting-
off act—she'd been chosen, you know, Out There, by
some kind of celestial lottery, to take the shape that Joe
found so appealing and mend the human condition.

The owner was off looking for a new ALS in Nova
Scotia and things got strained in the barn, but the G.'s
were only there sporadically and couldn't be bothered
with quarrels on that level. They just stopped credit at
the store, enjoyed their skiing and didn't think too much
about the gas bill until Mike dropped in and remarked on
its being also from Outer Space. Then it was the electricity. Then the telephone. Joe had done a very inge-
nious job hooking into all three.

We were down there with the family one afternoon
after skiing and he came in to borrow a quart of milk.
This was a day or two before he and what's her name—
Antigone, was it?—went off to take possession of their
share of the Southwest, so the G.'s were keeping their
cool, all five of them, and Joe was in fine form even
though he'd failed the day before to sell the twelve-year-
old on LSD. "You know it's hard to believe," he said with
the beatific puzzlement he frequently fell into, "how
many people like really don't understand the power of
love. I rack my brains over how that can be and I just

don't get it. An obvious thing like that, like any b-baby
can see it, and they act like they never heard of it. Like
I mean B-Beethoven, Mahler, Woody Guthrie, that's all
love music, that's what makes it real, and like can you
imagine anybody not recognizing a s-simple thing like
that?"

He went off with the milk and a big new can of peanuts
he'd caught sight of too, humming "This Land Is My
Land."

This commonplace episode is redeemed by a certain
effect of light that occurred during it. I've said the G.'s
are extremely goodlooking but not in what way, though
I did mention Apollo and Aphrodite in that connection,
which gives an idea. Only our friends haven't the rather
forbidding classic Greek profile. There's a dip between
forehead and nose, though each feature separately could
be off the Parthenon. I was particularly aware of the fact
that afternoon because the older boy, majoring in classics,
had left a book on the couch, open to a reproduction of
a vase painting. The subject was a banquet of the gods,
who had apparently left off their bickering for the party
and although hardly as merry in expression as we all were
before Joe came in, did have a striking resemblance to the
G.'s, in features as in poise. The mother has a rounder face
than her husband and two older children and is the only
one of the five not above ordinary height. They all move
with a grace not at all feline, more like that of enormous,
courteous flowers, able to move about or as on this occasion sit in various relaxed stances, smiling pleasantly, as
though neither grievances nor chores to be done had any
part in their existence.

They were still in ski clothes, boots off; had skied hard
all day, very fast as always, and were weary. The furni-

ture was crumbum maple, two-burner stove in corner, broken-down studio couch to be opened at night for two to sleep on, ragged Indian spread, other near-rags for curtains—fairly typical skiers' pad. The girl, a passionate sailor and student of oceanography, needing no hair to frame her marvelous beauty, wears it pulled back with ultra-severity into a blond pony-tail. Her teeth are dazzling in smiles or laughter, but just then she was flopped on the couch with a coke, feet on table, and was not exactly smiling. None of them was, except around the eyes. Neither friendly nor critical, nor even polite except by habit, they seemed all brought to a sudden mysterious cessation of response of any kind, by the appearance of some grotesque but harmless mythical animal in their midst, instead of a character by then only too familiar in both methods and rhetoric.

What happened must have, I'm sure, some natural explanation, perhaps related to the amount of space in the small room taken up by those extra-tall people and the intensity, all brought to one focus, of their thoughts and very large grey eyes. For lights there were only two or three cheap table-lamps, with battered paper shades; they were not responsible, and the few cars that passed didn't cast their beams in the windows as high-powered ones might have. An illumination began spreading, slowly, from what seemed to be all parts of the room, like *son et lumière* but without visible source, unless conceivably the open page of the book, and not French, I just don't know the Greek for it. It was the gods at the banquet, five of them, come to life on their vase, yes, and at the same time very far away from it, half flesh half clay and all radiance, arrested in mid-transformation by a sheer attack of bemusement at the human spectacle. At least that's the way it looked to me, and must have to Joe too. I had never heard him stutter before, and although he remembered his two bits of loot it must have cost him an effort. He had begun looking for once rather unsure of himself and his exit was uncharacteristic in two respects; his stride was something less than imperious, and he was humming badly off key.

The next instant, amid big changes of posture and comic glances of comment and relief, the light was back to its previous wattage.

Of last night's overnight company how very endearing one is, to us all—ageless courageous man still slim and strong in body, young in face too for all the brown ravage gutting such handsomeness, humor rescued alive from terrible wrecks and ditches, mistakes in life, wrong turnings, from which he has made his way like some shipwrecked sailor of long ago to the toughest of new starts. A whole new life taken up *nel mezzo del cammin;* job without status or much pay among—well, my old youthful idea of the leper colony, something like it but without even that drama for support: among young people so needy they can't even know their need or that he is anything but a fool or failure or profiteer of some incomprehensible kind to be spending himself among them. One way he will never be funny is in ridicule, of them or anyone—almost anyone; sardonic he can be, about the foibles and felonies we all agree on but even that's muted, since he totally lacks, it seems, the so general need of somebody to slash or blame. And his honesty and lack of pretension, along with that running wit, are so truly strange and rare, more worldly friends meeting him here act quite bewildered by it, not knowing if he's a genius in mufti or Dostoievski's idiot that we've picked up somewhere. He's neither—just an unusually civilized person.

So just family alone again for a few days, first time since the flood, and how delicious that is too. I forgot to say the laundry line is exceedingly high, put up originally for boat sails—from upstairs porch to way up in a big maple—and that's why the sheets can wave so beautifully, no doubling to cramp their swing or mar the patterns of sunlight. A stiff wind has risen, making another wild chase of tree-shadows as sharp as the sheets.

Now in this fullness of light and leisure, no particular press for dinner or anything, am torn between thoughts and items. If there's a distinction. Maybe they're all stories. They seem to have the same kind of insistence and urgency, the same the brook has right now too in its Houdini speeds and skills in afternoon brightness, down in front of the cabin where the old black kitchen range is, with the copper wash-boiler on it for no special reason except there's no other space for it and it looks nice there. The brook is not nearly so much a presence in the main house, it's so steep between, though close in sound at night; and here in this isolation cell, once a hunters' camp, across the road, I haven't got the brook at all. Just as well; I'd be at it all day, worse than TV. Perhaps it's because there's so little left of summer that I'm taken by a fearful appetite to understand the brook, see it all in every second's change, not miss a rock or eddy, swallow it whole if I could, make it part of me and me part of it forever. I love you I love you I love you is all I find to say to it. Not that we often do much better in our human infatuations.

Impatience in other ways; some leaves are already falling in this wind. Can't wait for Odysseus to get to Ithaca and be recognized by his dog and kill the suitors and all the rest of it, but we'll have to wait. Telemachus is just sneaking out at night to the ship to go look for him; a lot has to happen before we get him home, including a great change of expectations line by line on our part after the grip of the Iliad. Very different kettle of fish; same narrative pyrotechnics though—something else to wow about, brave astronauts!—what story-telling and by the same fellow, has to be, named Homer we hope. A very valuable world citizen in other ways he was too. Better than all our photographers art or press. Nobody else gives you those thrilling details—of how the food came to the table and where the table was between meals, and who put what fleece down where for a guest-bed, and exactly how pieces of armor were attached to corresponding parts of an anatomy, and how almost anything used was made, and at most tender length how to hitch a mule team to a wagon. There's the real sound and stuff of life; there's a poet; so send one to Mars only she/he had better be good, healthy too, none of your suicide-fanciers; and we'll see how that mule is harnessed.

But the story, what makes us care about the bits and pieces, that will be for some other millennium if it's not lost for good—that "once and for all" again, just to keep the underlying theme of this opus in mind as aesthetic discipline requires. (Over-all pattern, relation of parts to whole and parts to parts essential for dis-boring oneself or even effective KOFU; I do pour daily libations to the gods thereof.) Lost for now the sine qua nonsense of story certainly is. The renown of our heroes has the span of a fruit fly. Already the names are scarcely remembered of

those who first stepped on the moon; no Hector or
Achilles out there or in Vietnam; the closest to an epic
figure we get is Lt. Calley and that's just for mirror-value
(our Great Society etc.), not story. My Lai's no story,
neither will Mars be; there's nobody to hear it. Story-
telling is like fraud in business and politics—needs an
eager and understanding public, a whole social setup sym-
pathetic to it. We would need millions of mothers around
the evening lamplight telling their children all the marvelous and funny things that happened that day while they
were in the supermarket, or on the job if they have one,
and fathers ditto from office and bar-car, and stories from
their own childhoods and fairy tales.

But as the sad saying goes, let's fact it. Evenings have
fallen to TV and PTA and AA and Smokenders and
other gatherings worthy or therapeutic. Our heroes generally ride the ski-lift unrecognized, unsung; mythless we
bum, the rich like the far from it, around our shrunken
world, with no better than a Nixon or Manson or Patty
Hearst for brief negative reminders of once upon a time,
when stories were something to listen to and people did;
or later when they were written and were read. That's
how we know about the bored type in Russia, the social
climber in France, the sense of sin in New England. It's
not story-time any more, ever. People think you're defective if you tell one: not serious, have an anecdotal mind,
something wrong with your head. Verbally we're allowed two forms of discourse, reporting and arguing. In
written fiction the rules are narrowing down to plain and
fancy—no brains or nothing but. In the latter it's a point
of honor for the reader to pretend to be all agog over the
author's next cerebral pinwheel or sparkler; for sustaining
interest it's that or nothing. Same in theater. The game is

called Doctrinaire, gotten out by the makers of Monopoly etc., and is available at all better universities. Some play it in medieval costume; a favorite in intellectual periodicals.

I wonder if Homer's world ever looked so enormous and luxuriant as now against this dearth and drought. Every sea-breeze an excitement; distances, as from Crete to Troy, Ithaca to Pylos, enormous; real people engaged in real happenings, though the people may have one immortal parent and gods are always taking a hand in the events. What a thought-breeder, how your mind races through the whole story to fit the piece in the puzzle when Helen, back home with Menelaus now as if there were no memories though memories are the whole gist of the passage, speaks just in passing, between commas, of "the wanton that I was." Five words!

Come to think of it, it might be psychiatry as much as instant communication that has done for the story. If everything is to be explained and unraveled as you experience it or observe it in others there's nothing to be agog about. No suspense, everything predictable. So she ran off with another guy; so what; what do you expect, with those childhood influences. If your mother had conceived you by going to bed with a swan—who was really the king of the gods—you'd be flighty too and spend years with a shrink. She was rich enough, she could afford it. But that way would not have launched a thousand ships or any. True, she's less of a person than Clytemnestra or Penelope, but she's treated as one, she's no author's brainchild. Her trouble was being exceptionally beautiful and evidently not too bright in spite of her paternal lineage; and so the story is possible.

In general mortals with one immortal parent are a curious contrivance—to be taken just how literally? Must mull over it. Offhand I would think very little, just because we don't know people down the street of supernatural parentage and the original audience for these stories didn't either. But then the neighbors weren't considered interesting material. For a good story, the larger than life is a necessary ingredient, and you have to be made to believe it—the reverse of psychoanalyzing it.

Impulse faltering; this candle about burned out; was yesterday anyhow.

Not that hell again—those months of nothing. I couldn't; can't; won't.

Pascal on Montaigne—"Le sot projet qu'il a de se peindre." I'd hate to have to choose between those two. It would be fun though if there were some instrument to measure which of them has been of more benefit to people per century. All benefits to be included—amusement, illumination, practical guidance.

Memo: am not lonely, penniless, in pain, alcoholic or even overweight. Might be all of those some day, and totally blind or deaf too. Many people are, not just in old age, all or most of their lives. But then why ... And therein lies the basis of all religions. However, a clergyman who loves fishing is quoted as saying, "There is no clear line between trout-fishing and religion." Protestant, of course. It's really strange what people are willing to bear. Why? what's the point? they must ask themselves every day and never get an answer, yet they go on with it. A taboo—is that all? Or just the little physical fear of turning on the gas or the jump or the razor blade. Hope can't spring eternal, we know it doesn't. And in fact, speaking of the U.S.A., I wouldn't be surprised if the will to live were at its lowest ever in human history. Suicide rate no indication—a lot of people keep living who would prefer not to; crime figures tell more.

Item: the Hotel Lutétia in Paris, where my friend the professor of philosophy later had a room for the one-month wild springtime of his middle age, was taken over by the Gestapo during World War II. A young woman I had known slightly, as a girl and later with her fiancé —they were of the very correct upper bourgeoisie, only handsomer and more fun-loving than most—was summoned there one day for a meeting, so the German message said, with her husband. He had been picked up, for some resistance activity, and she had been without any news of him for a year. After she had been left alone for a while in an upstairs room, the side door opened and he came in, on his own feet. He had no idea who she was, had been made insane, and that was the point of having her go there to see him—a joke, or refinement. A few months later she was told where she could reclaim his body.

Nothing like that is ascribed to human beings in Homer. No torture, unless you count Odysseus' treatment of the treacherous goatherd, which is made to seem only too justified. No cruelty of any kind for its own sake; that is the prerogative of monsters. Killing is forthright, in battle or revenge, and the victor crows over the fallen, but there is no instance of a warrior inflicting a wound on purpose to make an opponent die slowly and protract his agony.

Louis XI, they say, enjoyed cruelty for its own sake,
and has been generally considered a monster. No doubt
with the craze for revision on, some historian will discover if they haven't already that he was kind and genial
as well as a brilliant statesman, but those cages he had
hung from ceilings and took such pleasure in are to be
seen at Loches. Such a pretty place; fine old castle and
peaceful, tilled countryside around.

It's an odd fact that we've never had dungeons in the
U.S.A. All kinds of jails and prisons of course and plenty
of nasty episodes, but the genuine dark clammy article
with stone walls a yard or more thick and the great iron
rings in the wall to chain the victims to, if we've had that
it can only have been some local aberration. Not federal
policy; we got going too late; not that dungeons were out
of style everywhere in the seventeenth century but it
took a while to get things going to that point and nobody
seems to have thought of building much with stone.
You'd think they would have, instead of these million
miles of stone walls we have here in the woods, but of
course the trees had to be cut and I suppose logs made
quicker work, for jails too; and perhaps dungeons had
unpleasant associations to some early settlers. So what
with one thing and another, and the absence of castles
except later on of the W. R. Hearst variety, they got left
out. Makes a peculiar heritage, for our middle-of-the-road
climate. Eskimos and South Sea Islanders have done without them for obvious reasons and they're no main attraction in Greece if there are any (Turkish? Venetian?) but

a dungeon or two a day is normal tourist fare in most of Europe. Not in a class with cathedrals for art or even architecture but very instructive in other ways, in spite of a certain monotony as between one and another. See one see all you might say but it's not quite true. In our American innocence we think of dungeons as deep underground whereas most on the contrary are high up in a tower—not even a *donjon* which generally meant an armory—and the view the prisoner could not see and the suicide leap he was unable to make varied greatly. This somewhat changes the imaginative nature of his experience and ours. Furthermore very different chunks of history are involved, with only the brute fact of power over an enemy as a common denominator.

We didn't linger long in the fortress of Loches. I only single it out because it's the most recent of my dungeon excursions and the visit happened to occur on one of these honey-lit September days like those we're entering on now—the kind of weather that makes lights and shadows and all impressions strike deeper than usual. Didn't even pay the extra few francs to see the famous cages. No need to; you read about them, you know they're there, around another corridor or two, up a different flight of deep-worn stone stairs; given proximity and the right light and mood, imagination does better than guides. Didn't see the chains either and will never forget them; probably they were taken for other purposes ages ago. What you see is the walls and the awful rings in the walls that one end of the chain was attached to, and a height worse than the World Trade Center, since a main factor in all dimensions is the feeling aroused and nobody but the hard-pressed rental agent gives a damn about all those offices. What goes on in them is exactly the same as if they were anywhere else, high or low, not at all the case with Loches.

You need no fear of heights to have your breath come short on those top turrets, over the wide spread of mellow fields forever rehearsing their clang of battles past.

In terror you enter the high dungeon room, let your thin-soled sandals down on the stones where Ludovico il Moro, of the great Sforzas of Milan, lay or paced barefoot for seven years. A lesson in luck; he'd have done the same to the king if he could. Summer, winter, seven times; he scratched words on the wall; whatever garments they gave him must have been foul, the bowl of food to be imagined. The old story. Wires were pulled, the thing by strenuous diplomacy arranged at last. He was unchained, led down the many narrow stairs, and on the drawbridge, we are told, at the sight of his freedom, fell dead. The change was too much for him. The children of Loches have presumably been playing Louis and Ludovico ever since, with paper chains if nobody has real ones to spare.

Yes, clearly, growing up with a genuine dungeon in your back yard would be a fortifying experience. At the very least it must inculcate a feeling about the laws of chance and the blows of fate rather less flimsy than most of ours, whereby every pain or calamity is unjust, a denial of our sacred right to the pursuit of happiness. True, we've had chaingangs in some parts of the country, a rather backward form of punishment, but in theory at least for certain stipulated offenses—not the throw of the dice that most good dungeons represent and that does so much in the formation of a mature personality. Around here the only chains, since wagons went out, are for hauling vehicles stuck in mud or snow, or serve briefly to guard the entrance to a "vacation home." Briefly because they'll be hacksawed off and stolen almost at once, like woodpiles and anything else that might come in handy. When leading citizens are thieves, it's only right for the less fortunate to copy them on whatever level they can.

For stones, aside from brookbeds and walls once marking fields—now fragments of a strange calligraphy waiting in woodland for the last erasures—or those in an occasional meadow that never got cleared except by cattle or sheep, we have one architectural phenomenon. No, two. Cellar-holes, and the walls of dug wells. Scattered all through the woods on the lower shoulders of the mountain and down here by the stream where another few also mark the site of a mill. I was forgetting—there are gravestones too, very few for a long time after the westward push. Where a bit of roof lasted longer than usual over the cellar-hole you can still find a decayed section of cupboard, a bleached scrap of wallpaper, and in one of more recent date, a rain-washed letter about a woman member of the family in the insane asylum. That was a big house, higher and more lonely than most, burned down by a later generation for the insurance. The others may have left the kitchen door closed that last morning, and maybe somebody threw a penny or an old shoe for luck in the well, but you wouldn't say so to look at them now. They defy recollection. The people who had put their backs and hands into all that work with stone, not to mention the timber on top, seem to have vanished with no goodbye, like ghosts.

Still, as spooks they can't compare with some who are legally alive and now running bulldozers over those cellar-holes. Weekend hunters and snowmobilers, other part-timers in any season, drifters of all sorts—all the spin-off of our huge restless lightweight society. Owners of A-frames or condominium space for a little while—two or three years too long anywhere—but really car-dwellers.

The tide has turned, the trend's reversed, landsharks
dream of bright-trimmed chalets falling thick as sprinkles
on a birthday cake. A few quiet types survive in the
fallout, for the time being.

Two things to be said for Loches—it wasn't fly-by-
night and it bred no illusions. On the whole we in our
country don't like or at least approve of cruelty, or arbitrary power either although if you call it big money it can
get by until some nutty journalist or crusader starts spilling beans. So we've been unfair to dungeons. I don't even
like them myself. I enjoy saying what I want, and walking
out the door when I want to, as much as the next person;
the whole gulag idea and system are so little credit to our
race, it's enough to make you apply for legal status as a
monkey; with medicine where it's at, you'd probably have
no trouble growing the requisite suggestion of fur.

So all I mean is, such structures do have resonance.
Something happened in them; they weren't just car-stops.
And more than most habitations of stone, they ring with
a word we're the poorer for losing—WOE. No exclamation mark unless you add IS ME. Philological kinship to
WOW! uncertain but it seems no society can be children
of both, and our present national character obviously calls
for the one with the exclamation mark.

However, not being a native of Loches, nor inclined to
swell the current wave of expatriates, I'm settling happily
enough for the cellar-hole just outside a window of this
small cabin, and the well we discovered deep in underbrush up by the tennis court. It must have belonged with
the other cellar that's closer than this one and nearly
vanished now. The family down here probably used the
beautiful spring across the road that used to be all our
water supply too and recently had several truckloads of

rock, earth and waste tree-stuff dumped on it, as part of
a senseless widening of the road. I keep hoping it will
show up somewhere else, as mint beds do, but probably
it's had to make its way underground to the brook and
never will. Somebody—I wonder if it was the owners,
that day they started west, with perhaps a lot more sorrow than hope in their hearts—had thoughtfully pulled
two big flat stones for a roof over the well, to keep leaves
and small animals from falling in. We heave them off once
a year in June and let down a bucket to fill the roller, as
there's no running water near the tennis court, and the
resonance then is ever so much more than from the
bucket clanging against the stones.

For years afterwards I dreamed about the house, real
dreams in sleep, of ghostly return and wayward wishing,
and so I suppose some of the others must have too, from
that building and the others like it on the block. All cold-
water flats except the firehouse next to us, with a few little
ground-floor commercial places, Chinese laundry, bric-a-
brac store usually closed, one small eatery, and the cellar
kingdom of Joe the Italian—his father's really but young
Joe was the one we knew best because he did the carrying, providing most of us with ice and cannel coal. Nobody on the block had an electric refrigerator that I ever
heard of, though this was after World War II. "Too old
to dream"—there's a fraud of a phrase for you. Mr. Santini must have been the fiercest dreamer of us all if the
move didn't kill him, but I expect it did. He was the last
holdout.

When I moved into the top floor east, just above him,

he still had his workshop a block away, not for much longer though and it was an awful blow to him to give it up. He sold his big tools and moved the small ones into the front room of the flat, southern and sunny but an extra expense to heat; mostly we all lived in our kitchens in winter. Still, even then he would bundle up and I would hear the cheerful buzzing and whirring of his trade, a companionable sound. Even if he'd had the right contacts, I suppose people weren't buying his kind of cabinetwork any more and you could see why, marvelous though it was. He showed me what he had there as we got to be friends. He couldn't stand being idle and he was a virtuoso with wood, all kinds—cherry, mahogany, teak, beautiful scraps he must have saved from better days, in inlays so fine and perfectly joined you'd think he'd have needed a microscope for the work, but his taste was of another time and place and nobody bought. It would be all rose petals and girls with castanets, not painted you understand but carved and glued, in lovely shades of wood.

The rent was $23 a month until the last couple of years when it went up to $26. He'd lived there on the third floor many years, with his wife until she died and now he had a nice Irish ladyfriend who didn't live there but came every day. When I happened on the house several flats were empty, something to do with recent change of ownership, but the agent may have blinked a bit to let Mr. Santini and one or two other tenants hang on when the building was supposed to be vacated, maybe for a new boiler being installed. If the stairs were repaired there was no sign of it, except for the extraordinary fact that they never did give way, even under the Countess's parties. Mr. Santini had no children, only a bad nephew who was after him for money and would cause loud outbursts of Italian

rage down there once in a while. Mostly the sounds that
came up the areaway were pleasant, of ordinary talk or
the tools or him singing to himself, along with the little
radio that was usually on but never too loud. In summer
lots of other sounds, especially across the blighted space
in back beyond our fire escapes, were much louder. It's
funny to think we never worried about anybody coming
up the fire escapes, or on my story from the lower roof
next door, only a step from my bed, or about answering
the doorbell either. It would be Joe with the ice, or a
friend, and quite often Bible tract people and the Fuller
brush man who did far better business there than among
the rich. It's only a wonder we didn't go up in flames, with
the heaters we used, but in seven years the firemen next
door only had to come to retrieve a dying kitten that had
fallen down the areaway, and to carry my father up to
the top floor for Thanksgiving dinner, because of his
breathing trouble that now would probably be called
emphysema. The bell clanging and siren shrieking peri-
odically when they set off for a fire somewhere else were
comforting noises, except as we were too accustomed to
register them at all; you felt in good hands, in case of need,
as Mr. Santini did about his little statue of the Madonna.
But then for all the fights you could see and hear across
that back wasteland in summer when city tempers get
high we never did hear of any robbery on the block—that
was for sections either better or worse, some very near—
or God forbid any muggings or murders.

The 3rd Ave. El half a block west gave a nice kind of
music too, of the trains passing, people joggling along in
the common enterprise of getting somewhere, staying
alive some way or other, and in sunlight or streetlight on
snow it made patterns as exciting as Mr. Santini's cabinet-

work when you managed to see lines in that instead of the calendar pictures.

The big house rumpus at times would be from the janitor's flat, second floor west, where shapeless, loud, lusty Mrs. McCullough, untidy of hair as in her epithets, for a while kept some sort of control over her five children and frequently drunk husband. Indeed she loved her children, without any grandiose hope of what's known as the best for them, and washed their clothes, for parochial school, a lot oftener than her own, that last being a bargain-basement cotton garment flung on as though in crisis, to be changed shortly instead of slept and otherwise lived in for the next week or two. Mr. McCullough too when sober could enjoy a good round of family jokes. There was laughter as often as dishes flying behind their door. I will say for him too, although he let her clean the stairs and sometimes shovel snow out front, he kept the hot water going. It was splendid, the term cold-water flat as everybody used to know meaning just no central heating. It must have been an obsession with him, making up no doubt for big failures in life, and the second wonder of the building was that the boiler never exploded.

Of course we all had the same floor plan, only in mirror-image as between east and west; sink doubling as washbasin in tiny space beyond kitchen; little bathtub with iron claw-feet beside sink with tin cover down except at bath-time, very handy for the dishes; and separate toilet cubicle at the back. In this last we were extravagantly lucky, most flats with the same rent having a shared toilet off the stairwell. The McCulloughs had one toothbrush for the seven of them and the baby threw it down the toilet so then there was none; no toilet either for quite a while, the toothbrush causing it to back up and overflow. The windows needed a lot of putty but the chimneys front and back were a marvel, that is they drew well without ever being cleaned or having been that I could discover, and the parlor ceilings were adorned with period plasterwork of good style, the rosettes and curlicues suggesting a bygone decorum quite soothing to think of. Of my own paint job and furnishings in the front room, Mrs. McC. was generous in her admiration, their equivalent being mainly a dumping space. "You've got it all ready for the groom to come in!" she said, but she didn't know her fairy tales. That was to take seven years and another coat of paint.

We had a right, each tenant, to a bin in the cellar and the first winter Mrs. McC. helped me clean mine out to store coal and firewood. She did it in hope of coming across something useful, and from the filthy dark we did haul out a dilapidated crib that she had trouble deciding about; she wasn't planning on any more children. "Five I already gave that skunk . . ." Her large wavering circumference outlined a massive sponge soaking up a hundred years of cellar history as she pondered a second, the longest she ever thought over anything. But the crib was better than nothing. She kept it, going on about the elegant French widow who'd had the nerve to rent *two* flats and was driving us all crazy that year, with her parties and her spike heels on the wooden stairs at all hours. There hadn't been two free on the same floor so she took, for my sins, the one next to me and the one below that. She was hard up for the moment and thought it would be a lark to move over from Park Ave.; I never let on to Mrs. McC. that it was my fault in a way, through a friend of mine who was one of her lovers at the time and told her about the house. On her third-floor door she put up a calling card big as a wedding invitation, La Comtesse So-and-so, and she didn't understand that you took your own garbage down to the street, or more likely that was just carrying the lark too far. She expected the McC.'s, for tips, to do that and a lot else for her. They were to be a combination concierge and peasant family on her estate, available for any need or whim, at all hours. "That count she's a son of a bitch," Mrs. McC. said as we emerged from whatever soot wasn't stuck to our persons, and her relations with the upper crust deteriorated from there. But then things were opening up again in France, that is the deceased count's bank assets were, so the merry widow left us and for years after friends of hers from the art world were coming by to move out huge items of furniture that she would cable them about. I had been away when she moved in and never could see how the things were gotten up the narrow sagging stairs in the first place.

Her successor on the top floor was a nice quiet college instructor with a pretty girlfriend he eventually married, and the only strain was from the impression at times that we were in the same bathtub together. Separated in the middle by the stairwell, the flats were cheek by jowl in the sinkroom, with the kind of walls you'd expect. Now he's reaching for the soap or the stopper—nope, changed his mind; and what was *that* splash about? don't tell me you lie on your stomach in a thing this size with your heels in the air. It was still more intimate when the two of them somehow got in together, in a form of sex-play not designed for that vintage of plumbing. Or he'd be bathing alone and would call to her way down at the street end of the flat, "Hey! I cut my toenails yesterday! yeah, hadn't done it for a couple of weeks." We would all nod courteously when we passed on the stairs and we exchanged formal wedding announcements later on.

In general there was not much fraternizing in the house. The two couples on the ground floor were poor, elderly, law-abiding, and one pair, the Nowells, were also flattened by grief, having lost their only son in the war. Besides us on the top floor, the only other non-proletarian element was below Mr. Santini, a scene of frenetic turn-over, the lease being handed on through a chain of unstable characters with scarcely any change of furniture; such as that was, nobody was in any condition to bother or remember who owned it. One young woman in the series, who had walked out on her two children, was found half dead there one day, with 26 pairs of shoes and 85 lipsticks around in the ghastly disorder. She had withdrawn from any friends she might have had and finally couldn't make herself go out to buy food. The darkness must have made it worse, daylight being progressively less on the lower floors. From my windows I could see to the East River and miles north and south and the light was marvelous all through. There were several pigeon-fanciers—keepers? farmers?—I used to watch on their roofs, waving long sticks to make their flocks fly off and multiply by attracting strays, or so it was explained to me, and when in early 1949 I came back from over a year in Italy I thought New York had gone pigeon-crazy. I was seeing thousands of perches. Nobody had written me about television coming in just then, or about frozen orange juice either; my sublet friends left me a can, with a note about its being something new; I thought you drank it straight, and was depressed.

The same friends had done some sub-subletting of their own, not quite on the pattern of the third floor but it did cause my only trouble with Mr. Santini. The girl in that case was defective only in never having seen an icebox like that and not being able to put two and two together, i.e. when the pan at the bottom got full you emptied it. Mr. Santini came roaring up because his ceiling was dripping, in fact collapsing by the time he found her in. Then she couldn't make the connection between pan and sink, so threw the water next time down the fire escape, into the pot of spaghetti sauce he had put out to cool. He forgave me if not her and went back to catching me on the stairs to offer me some of his excellent coffee sherbet, *granita di caffè con panna*; early on I'd said I loved it and admired his, so I was often stuck with it on return from a full dinner or at other awkward times. He spoke to me in the hybrid remains of his Italian, and as he couldn't do that with his Irish ladyfriend, and we were in general poised anomalously between Czechs to the south and Germans and Hungarians to the north, it was important to him. His situation on the whole was rather lonely anyway—of course he'd wanted children but his wife couldn't, something had been wrong; certainly his life lacked the sociability of its beginning in the Abruzzi, or of many Italo-American enclaves. He couldn't think of going back to Italy, had been away far too long, and perhaps the very excellence of his craft cut him off from some of his compatriots here. A few would come in for visits; not many. He was of an elite bound to be somewhat isolated, an artisan aloof from the common herd, confused with it by richer and better-educated Italians over by Lexington and Park where the Countess had lived. One night he woke me with a phone call at 3 A.M. to offer me a granita di caffè; he didn't even sound pleading or particularly urgent, only sad when I declined—"Peccato. Izza

too bad. Izza buona granita. I make-a oggi"—and I
learned only a week later that he had been truly desperate
for company that night. He'd had what he took to be a
heart attack and thought he was dying, but was too proud
to say so.

Farther downstairs trouble developed, at the McCulloughs'. At sixteen the oldest child, a boy, began disappearing; they were tight-lipped about it, but his last
appearance at the old homestead was rather startling. He
arrived in a new tight-waisted suit and two-tone shoes,
pomaded hair cut to a swallowtail, in a yellow Buick
convertible that drew quite a crowd of wonderers while
it was parked out front; it made my little ten-year-old
Ford in the next space look like an alley cat. He dashed
upstairs, evidently after some belonging or other though
heaven knows what that could have been, had a howling
row that shook the poor old building to the roof, and was
gone, as far as I know for good. He might even have come
to give them money and whatever the mysterious source
of it was they cursed him instead; and perhaps the father,
drunk or not, beat him up too; he could have done it,
being of much huskier build; the boy was thin-boned,
shorter than either parent, resentful of glance and sallow
of complexion.

Not long after, late on a winter afternoon, I came home
to find their door open onto the stairwell exposing a scene
fit for Dickens. However, at the moment the excitement
of novelty was making the children sound more euphoric
than stricken. Under the one bare ceiling light-bulb the
oldest girl, about thirteen, was on a broken kitchen chair
trying to quiet her four-year-old brother. The stove had
gone out; the bedsheets in the adjoining cubicle, where
the parents slept with the little boy, were grimy and half

on the floor. I knew the three girls slept in one rickety bed in the wasp-waist section beyond, a clothes closet to me upstairs, and the departed prodigal had slept in the freezing junkroom designed as parlor, over the street. It seemed that Mrs. McCullough had used a neighbor's telephone to call an ambulance and had herself taken to a hospital an hour or two before, the girls weren't clear what for except she felt bad and had a pain; mainly, I think, she just couldn't stand the whole business another minute. For one thing, the gas had been turned off. They had no idea where their father was or when he might come. So pretty soon there were a few of us there, the Nowells from downstairs and the janitor's wife next door and even Mr. Santini who didn't normally mix like that, and we got the pot-belly going and brought food and called the priests who were used to such plights, and so the McCulloughs vanished that very night from our lives. The children were whisked to various orphanages and it always bothered me that the little girls hadn't been able to stay together. They were so used to sleeping in a huddle, when I had taken them for a week to my mother's house in Connecticut they had cried in terror the first night until we put them in the same narrow bed. A rather colorless new janitor couple moved in briefly.

The axe fell soon after. The whole block was to be torn down and the city gave us $1,000 per lease to get out, which seems to have been cheaper than relocating people. It was a huge sum and all but Mr. Santini accepted it, finding what other solutions they could, none happy, all more expensive. I should except myself, as life was smiling on me then in all other respects, yet the communal blow was heavy just the same. In deep ways we were in tatters. It hadn't been a particularly cordial house or block, peo-

ple weren't suspicious but they were pretty separate, nobody had ever tried to cook up a dance on our street; still,
familiarity breeds more than you know when it's in process. It was like a multi-party divorce hitting us, with
reasons and blame beyond understanding. All down the
street we began avoiding looking at each other; it was as
if we all shared some huge, horrid guilt; I suppose the
guilt really was that we were already in training for vio-
lating our own memories, wiping out all those years of
our lives, because we would dream about them and were
afraid of our dreams. Joe had stopped smiling and kept his
eyes lowered in the kitchens he knew so well; nice life,
nice people, he knew everybody, it suited him. Years
before he had said that his cousins, not necessarily in the
Mafia, had told him he should be more ambitious, but he
couldn't see why and now he had a beautiful bride who
agreed with him and was satisfied with what he earned.
It would have been too sad to remark that cannel coal and
block ice belonged in the same vanishing world with the
buildings and the odd safety we had enjoyed in spite of
everything.

No more smiles and hellos to the firemen lolling at the
station door between calls. Willy-nilly, being on city pay,
they were on the side of destruction, and looked embarrassed, almost hostile. We used to joke about their being
on the wrong side of us on the one-way street so if we'd
had a fire they'd have had go all the way around the
block. Now it didn't look as if they'd have bothered coming at all; because our quarters were condemned we had
become non-people, suddenly worthless.

Mr. Santini was nearly crying all the time in those days.
"They say they senda me to a project"—word of ana-
thema, he spat from his very soul over it. "I say can I put

a nail in the wall in your project? They say no. I say okay, how I live where I can'ta put a nail in the wall? I aska you, you call that a life, macchè vita, a man can'ta use a hammer in his own house, a casa sua! And the rent? Oh jezza leedla settanta ottanta dollari a month they say, you like it fine. I spit on them. Plaah!" He spat. He had aged terribly in a few weeks and his eyes blazed.

The last time I went by, the other front windows were all boarded up and his had been too, but a board had been pried up and I was sure he was peering out. Our rent collector had told me he was still there. The water and electricity had been stopped a week before and the street door was bolted so I couldn't go up to see him. I scarcely had the heart to anyway. Our long association, with all its uncrossed thresholds and delicate proprieties, felt fake and rather silly as against such extremity, and he couldn't have been making any more granita di caffè. Perhaps at the end he went at them with his wonderful chisels before they overpowered him, and perhaps our old friends at the firehouse, however reluctantly—and however impure their reluctance, like most people's in an act of violence —had to lend a hand in that last eviction. I've wondered many years about that, and where he went, and what his dreams were like at the end.

Our philosopher friend the other evening, in the lovely isolation and simplicity he and his wife have long been rooted in, half an hour away, defined the purpose of philosophy as the search for the Good. I argued that that was only ethics, and indeed I think he would agree that he is altogether secular in thought. First Cause (or Causes:

singular or plural according to your tradition and personal make-up) he calls a matter for science, not philosophy. Ebullient and life-loving by nature, he has come temperamentally as well as logically by his contempt for religion, though being also very kindly he wouldn't try to rob anyone of it who needed that comfort. Some truths, he maintains, are better left untold; hard to disagree with that. But quite a few that seem to me of shadowy or mixed category are for him civics and sociology. So on affliction—why under certain circumstances is it to be borne, etc.—we get around to voluntary euthanasia, and leave the disagreement there. A friendly and by no means total one anyhow. And of course he was quite aware of what prompted the probe, after many years of merely personal and political exchange. Such conversations, when as pleasant as that one, have rather the character of hummingbirds trying the heart of one blossom after another.

Saw new scenes of the recent flood damage on the way there—a flimsy bridge replacement had been put up only that day or we'd have had to drive across a ford or many miles around by a network of dirt mountain roads even the native-born get lost on if they've had a few drinks, not an uncommon condition. Also a few days before, visiting the great scholar of art history and his wife, perched by the remaining half of their little road, on the brink of a perilous drop, where for some forty years they had enjoyed a row of majestic maples bordering the stream. Farther up the same road several houses had been carried away: that's the expression, as if they would turn up bobbing around intact at sea some day. Really they just get toppled and smashed in varying degrees by uprooted trees and boulders on the march, ending up as caricatures of their old shapes caught in a grove or teetering on a bank a little way downstream. Like inhabitants of nursing homes, suddenly ugly and useless, their mementoes, accumulations of a lifetime, either dispersed or by loss of context turned to junk.

What endures of the old-time population around here tends to be generous in a pinch, means permitting, and seems to have some influence, in that way and others, on those few of the newcomers who last long enough to learn anybody's name. For those dehoused families a collection was taken up, apparently with no questions asked about insurance policies, although after a fire in the neighborhood once a similar beneficiary burst forth with a new car and truck and farm machinery such as none of the donors could afford.

Home auctions after a death have a similar air of desolation and meaning fled—on back road or village street here nowadays the substance gone each time from a lot more than a single individual's or family's possessions, poor things yanked from all that gave them honor. With each crockery teapot and painted rocking-chair there goes a little lifeblood from what used to be a community. The buyers are from out of town, derision or acquisition their moods; hardly anyone there knew the old geezer or knows any bit of the life story of the house, which will most likely be bought by weekenders and soon sold to others at a stiff profit when they get tired of it. Flood is a more dignified way of death for a house than that; so is lightning, which has done in quite a few homesteads, as they used to be called, in the vicinity.

But old Rob Blaine's place where the auction was last summer still has the For Sale sign up. I suppose the heirs are asking too much. Quite a few places around are

named for the family, a road and prize waterfall and a big
spread of scrub and old beaver-swamp known as the
Blaine Job, and what anywhere else would be a lake but
in the traditional understatement of this state is known as
Blaine Pond. (The pride of modesty in such namings will
of course die out as the new realtors get their way; real
ponds are now becoming lakes and any camp a home,
even if secondary.) The flowers are overgrown this year,
but what looks emptier even than the house is the space
in front of the barn across the road where he parked his
gorgeous yellow payloader when he wasn't riding it to or
on some job or other, with the mien of a Roman emperor
—one of the Antonines. Way up in his eighties—we'd
been to his golden-wedding party in the Town Hall some
years before—and never would consider not working,
except, they say, under pressure from his wife who badg-
ered him for sixty years to take her out driving; one time
it was to Alaska, the only holiday of their lives and a
busman's one at least for climate. He kept that exaspera-
tion private, as he did whatever others he felt in his many
years as selectman, in which role he would sit through an
evening's worth of proposed iniquities, betraying no opinion pro or con, to wind up in his nasal, noncommital
drawl, "I ain't seen those charts you were to bring along,
kind of high for sewage absorption by my figgerin'," or
"Nope. I guess I won't go along with that." His wife died
first and true romance quickly ensued, so the last two or
three years, after a day out on his high chariot he was
often to be seen, mirabile dictu, sitting, actually just plain
sitting, in a rocking-chair on the porch, holding hands
with the elderly widow-lady who had taught him, equally
marvelous to relate, to smile.

     It was nice weather the day of the auction, so it was

held outside on the mown grass, not exactly a lawn, toward the back of the house. The rows of public-utility chairs were incongruous as in a dream, and the cars parked for half a mile along the road nearly all had out-of-state plates. Our present five selectmen, who are doing so much for progress and prosperity, are also all from out of state, though of course legal residents for the moment. Same story, one gathers, pretty much all over and plenty of natives voting for it. They can't all be Rob Blaines, or born woodsmen like Harry, our nearest permanent neighbor, or in love with poverty and solitude.

The fool beavers—goddam beavers Harry calls them and he's trapped plenty, he should know—have built their dam again right back in the same place, not a hundred yards upstream from the cabin, where they'd already destroyed no end of trees. Over and over they've been washed out there, any spring freshet will do it, and even this last flood didn't teach them anything; when they move on it will be from some different logic altogether. Still you can't help admiring their toothmarks on any particular log and it's too bad we've made them such a scurrilous synonym. They're no more over-eager in their work than porcupines for instance, only more communal about it. It's not easy being any kind of wild animal; they all work hard, except in zoos, our version of Loches for them, with the torture of idleness.

According to our philosopher friend, treasure in mind and nature that he is, "What is the meaning of life?" is a non-question—I think he means because unanswerable, except in terms of religion. But then I would say philosophy has missed the boat. Give it another label. Call it logic, civics, methodology, something; disband the department; take it out of the curriculum. Who needs a

philosophy that doesn't ask the meaning of life but only
how to lead a good one? But oh well, I suppose if I were
teaching it I'd come around to that too. As daily fare it's
true the unanswerable would get tiresome. It's only interesting as an occasional exercise, like whacking at tennis
balls you can't see.

    How smartly September comes in, like a racing gig,
all style, no confusion. Here we are, folks, out with the
woolens. Pond cold, light sharp—you could cut trees, sky
and all with scissors, anywhere, late last night too when
the full moon came crashing up and it was another deluge
but of light, sudden and appalling—an instantaneous
white forest fire broken out everywhere at once. How
curious that there's so little weather in Homer, except at
sea.
    Today hiked up the mountain, two of us and our two
young visiting cousins—an hour and three quarters up,
hour and a half down. Same sharp light as now, making
pitch shadows in woods most of the time; occasional fast
clouds bringing spells of chill; brisk wind, colder, on top
of the fire tower where the young couple, of "creative"
bent, have kept watch in the six-month danger season, for
several years. They live in the cabin beside the tower, on
provisions packed up on their backs every week or two
though they've induced a few rows of lettuce to grow up
there. Chips carpet the yard from his tall wood sculp-
tures, started from found shapes in the woods, a lonesome
gallery, informed by the passage of Henry Moore once
on eagle-back, who knows how long ago. At least as informed as many in New York and perhaps not more

lonely, figuring in real weight and value. Friends do pack up for visits now and then; in the ALS turnover there are always a few of like mind. Bookish, disciplined in odd channels, keeping body and soul together by the barest, indulgent sometimes in mutual or self-appraisal, as many must have been who never quite made it to the point of getting themselves remembered among 4th Century saints: the holy failure list, yet in behavior, looks and conviction all Jeromes. Some come to be stalked by despair and have at times in their eyes the look of exhausted deer in hunting season. One of true gifts, in her twenties, admired for occult powers, is conversant with evil spirits although herself in no way wicked, and sees strange significant flames; no criticism may attend her thousands of unpublished pages and other painted thousands unseen outside the true-believing circle; her white fingers writhe in speech like long animated roots scarcely tolerating the light of day; her current kick is expecting to die soon and she has in fact managed to become deathly pale.

On a good summer day another kind of company, all sorts of hikers, reach the fire tower and usually sit there a few minutes to rest after the climb, and once in a while the keeper-couple may find a congenial soul among them, though statistically the chances are against it and they are too smart to hang out any standing offer of hospitality. The path rejoins the Long Trail a few miles below and humanly that is no longer always pleasant or even safe, or quiet, though in stretches and out of season still beautiful. The shelters in the prettiest places began to be so abused a few years ago, by drifters posing as hikers, taking them over by way of free lodging for weeks at a time, rangers had to be posted by them to take ID's and check dates of arrival and departure—a subway station, hideously in-

fected with trees and a dirty mirage of a lake, minus any
music of breeze or bird however, unless for a short time
before dawn when transistors might be stilled. We
stopped our overnight treks, but the baddies, noise-pollut-
ers and criminal types in general, seem to avoid the
tougher alternate route over the summit. It was mostly
family groups we met yesterday and not many of those
in spite of the Labor Day array of locked cars down by
the Blaine Job. The tower on its thin metal understruc-
ture sways in the wind, so do the many mountains seen
from there, crest after crest, sea upon sea, rocked in their
taunt of time: our accusers, our deep marriage beds. Ferns
frost-blasted the top mile or two, as also down here today,
but the many mosses that grow on that slope were in
luxury from the summer's dousings, miniature forests in
profusion; on a patch the size of your hand Odysseus and
all his shipmates or you and yours could lie down and
dream of no other homeland, it would be such sweet
sleep, under the immensity of specklings, yellow, lavender
and white, of the tall fall wildflowers in bloom. The Cyclops, the terrible cannibals, Circe are nearby—mountain-
country characters all, though of mountains rising from
the sea in that version—but our mosses here can be
stronger enchantment than any of them if you put your
face down close and breathe deep.

There was one character on the Long Trail one time
we didn't feel so sure about, moss or no moss, but it must
have worked. We got rid of him in the end, without any
of us being devoured or turned to swine, though it was
touch and go for a while. We were still going overnight
at that time, with rather heavy packs, because after a
strenuous day over bogs and hogbacks and such, stopping
only for wasp-stings, sprained ankles or a ripped cornea

from some wayward branch, we chose to reward ourselves in Homeric fashion with ample steaks and wine: no
spam or powdered chicken à la king for the master of this
house. We had dumped our gear, nine of us in a shelter
that could scarcely hold more, and most were off explor-
ing or fishing, when the monster came swinging down the
trail, causing our little black and white English cocker,
somewhat younger than he is now but no more lacking
in discretion—his grade has been zero in that subject right
along—to flounce around and yap rather energetically.
The man, if such he was, a solitary hiker anyway and
that's already suspicious, went livid, whether infuriated
more by the dog or because the only companion with me
at the moment was a black girl I don't know. Just then it
was the spaniel he took it out on, suddenly slipping the
towering pack from his back and with superhuman dex-
terity getting it into position to hurl, not as a simple
weapon in self-defense, but with exactly the rage of the
Cyclops throwing down the mountaintop, although we
had pushed no sharpened and burning lumber into his eye
nor at that stage even thought of it. The dog was scarcely
as high as his boot-tops, which scarcely covered his ankles, and of course by this time I was holding the dear
little thing and assuring the adversary he couldn't hurt a
flea—that was God's truth, he'd been trying all day without success—but it made no difference. "If he takes one
step toward me," bellowed the giant, who was perhaps
really of normal stature but to our eyes growing by the
second—perhaps we were seeing him from the dog's
point of view—"I'll kill him!"

And then I'll kill *you*, I wanted to yell back but thought
better of it, meanwhile backing toward the stones serving
as fireplace, where there lay a rusty iron rod used as a

poker by a succession of campers. He wasn't kidding, had
clearly been striding many miles over hill and swamp—
nothing you'd call a dale around there—nursing some
terrible, probably congenital rage and consumed with
hunger for something to take it out on. We and our dog
were just the ticket. So still glowering, abristle with ha-
tred, he moved in with us. That was the one shelter in the
section not open-sided, built for the purpose; formerly a
small refuge for hunters, it had four walls or approxima-
tions thereof each at its own rakish angle, four plank
shelves for beds, a little iron stove with a rickety pipe
wandering from it to a hole high in a wall, and a large
permanent population of mice. It could be very cozy in
congenial company, with the lake faintly lapping just
outside and sleep broken only by laughter of loons and
gnawing of porcupines under your bed if they hadn't
gotten to the bacon instead, or a mouse taking the shortest
route to a crumb, across your face. Also pleasant was the
custom in those days of replacing any firewood you had
used, for the next-comer, and burying your cans and garbage. But such consideration was already waning then
and the place was burned to the ground a year later by
some new-style occupants, who moved in for the entire
fall and didn't know how to handle that type of stove.

I remarked that the space was fully taken; he remarked
that there were only two of us; I remarked that the others
would be back soon. He strode wrathfully inside to count
the packs, and although they bore me out and then some,
dumped his in the doorway and proceeded to unpack pan,
can, can-opener and a change of socks. He was evidently
considering where to build his own fire and in what re-
ceptacle to carry his own water from the nearby spring,
and whether to bash the spaniel's brains out at once or

wait till we were asleep and he could cook him without interference, when I set up a hallooing across the lake to the rest of our party. Come back fast was the gist of it and luckily they heard, and answered. The answer part of it made the interloper a bit restless; it seemed he must have been weak at logical inference and hadn't visualized all those packs as connected with real people, some of them grown males at that; one of whom on grasping the situation pointed out in a mild tone that there were two other shelters, both unoccupied and also by the lake, a little way on.

No reply, and dusk came on, and in the darkening still water strange living shapes and voices not unfamiliar to the seething stranger began to make themselves felt. And not only there; at moments his ear was cocked and his lips formed a response in the direction of the black woods as well, while his fingers strummed on the hatchet between his knees. He sat or rather squatted on his haunches a few yards from our sociable if somewhat short just then of cheery circle. We forced out bad jokes and even a snatch of song, of the sort associated with campfires at happier times; the children fell into a convulsion of ghoulish laughter, as Hansel and Gretel probably did while waiting to be fattened up by the witch. A chipmunk's skittering brought little shrieks to our throats; we whirled to face any leaf that stirred. Not another word passed between us and that dark presence, too busy with his unearthly colloquy to light the tiny fire he had laid or open his spam. Or perhaps there was another reason. As long as possible we had delayed putting our great juicy steaks over the coals, but now in our famished state, just when we should have been most on guard—especially as the cocker had woken from his snooze and was straining at his leash—

their sizzle and aroma nearly turned our minds from dread. And then before we knew it the irate man, trembler before small dogs, hater of all fellow men, had hoisted his pack and was disappearing down the trail.

I believe some slight fragrance of moss clinging to one or another of us must have done it. At any rate his bosses or servants, whatever it was he had been communing with, quickly fled the scene too and the stars came out.

In all our years here there has been no serious forest fire nearby, I suppose because of the watch from the tower; during bad drought the arts suffer, somebody has to be up there all the time. But one night when Zeus had decided to end a long dry spell with some of his top-drawer thunderbolts, we woke at one in the morning to a powerful smell of smoke. The sky seemed afire and everything under it and we felt exceedingly fragile. But all that glare and flame was from a single dead pine, the tallest around, that had been struck by lightning, and after we had fetched Harry out of bed, that old master in the ways of the woods, and fought our way through underbrush toward the base of the fearful torch, he decided it would be all right, the lower growth around had gotten soaked enough not to catch. And he was right, though the crash and crackle continued and the red glare showed through our eyelids the rest of the night.

"By Jesus," fingering his pajama-top—he'd yanked on boots and pants though—"it picked a time, didn't it?" with the gravelly laugh combining friendly merriment with deep sardonic bite, whether at human folly of which he's a superb narrator, or the ways of fate. Aged seventy now, more wiry than husky to look at, slow-moving but still strong and speedy enough when required, Harry prefaces most of his remarks and stories that way, doubled with

"By God" or "By Christ" for special emphasis, in drollery or disgust. Beavers may call for it, or snowmobilers, or weekend hunters leaving a wounded animal, something his kind would never do. He's slept out often with his dog under balsam boughs in sub-zero weather and might be fool enough to risk it even now to keep tracking something he'd hit and not killed, and not just deer the family needed for the winter's meat. Or it might be the latest shenanigan of a certain fellow native, bully in the region and toady to the rich and powerful outside it. "So by Jesus," with that laugh, as if what he's about to recount had been perpetrated just for public amusement, "that bird pulls some wires somewhere and gets the contract and we're paying a hundred thousand for the damn fool thing instead of the fifty we voted, no goddam sense to it to begin with ..." It's in his mellowest mood he calls such a character "that bird." Harry himself has never had enough cash to worry about, nor disdain for any honest job when a little was needed. "By Jesus, I said to myself, a man doesn't have to be a slave ..." So had to find a wife, and did, who would relish her part of the bargain. His grey hair is kingly, growing up thick and high over the kind of forehead called intellectual, and his standing in the section would make it hard for the bird himself to return the compliment. There just aren't many outside the little cabal of sub-toadies, and their invisible gods of finance and they don't live here, who wouldn't naturally address Harry, if current custom permitted, as "Noble Harry, sir, son of Benjamin, master woodsman, trapper, tinker, carpenter, knower of the holiness of the wild, true artist of the peg-joint as of life ..."

In the morning he and Rob Blaine, then only about

seventy-nine, and another volunteer helped us put out the last of the fire.

The yellow is goldenrod of course, the lavender wild aster, the white I must look up—oh, I keep forgetting, I can't; will have to ask somebody. This wretched dependence! The steep-wooded rise across the brook is already shaded to burgundy and one stunted young maple under the window has jumped the gun and turned scarlet, a month before the big show and the "foliage traffic" that goes with it, when we won't be here. Ennie has kicked the virus at last; Prodge with heroic labor has finished his 26-ft. hull, all he can do or expected to this year. In a few days will have to get in firewood for ski-time, and take up the tennis-court tapes, and on his hill beyond the village old Larry Tippett, alone now since his brother died, with the grandest sugarbush around, will start laying in the far vaster wood supply he'll need for his two sugarhouses next March.

Still in trouble about music, that lifelong necessity. Curious feeling; like throat obstruction I imagine, making difficulty in swallowing. I resent its being pushed forward now, not by anybody, just by the situation, as such a different kind of necessity: lifesaver, alternative to what's lost. Secretly I yell No, no! and shut my ears, or they shut themselves. Will come around I suppose and get it back where it belongs, to being positive pleasure, not a bloody consolation.

Meanwhile, though, there's one song I do keep enjoying the thought of. I can't exactly sing it or hear it because it has no tune. In fact it's really a poem, dreamed by my

husband and he's a crackerjack dreamer; I don't mean he's
any slouch awake but that's when he hits the jackpot,
nearly every other night. It's called "The Girl I Mentioned." I spoke of it as a song because in the dream it was
accompanied by about a thousand swooning violins and
hundreds of beautifully dressed couples were also swooning with delight as they danced to it. The dreamer was
delighted too to have it so appreciated, and woke up in
a burst of laughter.

> *Things are falling apart,*
> *Things are drifting away,*
> *But the girl I mentioned*
> *Is in the middle of today.*
>
> *Things are falling apart,*
> *Things are crumbling to dust,*
> *But the girl I mentioned*
> *Is an absolute must.*

That gives me positive pleasure, even now at this sad
stage in the spiritual overhaul. I don't know if I'm the girl,
would like to think so, but of course for a work of art
such questions are irrelevant.

"Girl": American vernacular, like "kids," covering
practically indefinite age-span.

One camp, or cabin or vacation home, a mile and a
half up the road, belongs to some people we call the
Tidies. I've heard their real name many times but don't
remember it, because I can't think of them as anything but
that, and I wouldn't be surprised if they were down on
the tax list that way, though we've kept the name to
ourselves. It's just that there's no other way of thinking

of them so it seems as if everybody else must too. It's like
Aeolus being associated with the winds—no question
about that, everybody knew it—or think Persephone,
think pomegranate seeds and underworld, no two ways
about it. That's how it is with the Tidies; they're mythical;
they belong in an epic, but until the right bard comes
along I'll just have to do the best I can for them.

Being lord, lady and offspring of our contemporary
epoch, they have neither origins nor faces, unless perhaps
in one another's eyes—none that the rest of the world
could know. They're far too busy for that. I spoke of
them as a couple without thinking. I suppose they're that,
and that the children we've glimpsed assuming different
sizes over the years are theirs; as they never look up from
their labors when here, and couldn't take time for the
wave of the hand generally considered de rigueur in these
parts, that too would be hard to know. Must remember
to ask Harry; he gets to know everybody and can crack
the toughest nut, probably because he doesn't give a damn
if he does or not; if people want to tell him anything, fine,
and if not, that's fine too. Or perhaps I won't ask. Something less than mythical might come out.

As I said, all we ever see them do is work—not laugh
or smile or play ball or enjoy their handsome roadside
pool or relax, none of the things you'd think people
would have a weekend place in the woods for; just work,
and a most peculiar kind of work it is. They tidy up, and
tidy up, and then tidy up some more, until Sunday afternoon arrives and they close the tidy wooden shutters
provided for every single immaculate window and head
back to whatever other burdens life lays upon them,
wherever that may be, city or suburb, who can tell. Not
a line is out of plumb, not a weed survives, not a blade of

grass grows beyond correct lawn height on the tended
acre; the unclipped woods in back must give them night-
mares. In winter they don't come often but when they do
they step only in the short symmetrical path they dig
from car-park to front door, taking the same pains not to
mess up their snow as they do in the more Herculean job
of somehow whisking away every autumn leaf that has
the temerity to fall on their immediate premises. The
woodland of which they also own a parcel they must
resolve to keep strictly out of sight and mind in that
season, lest it send them screaming to the nearest highway.

This is not to imply any upper-income pretensions, not
at all. The house is small, really a cabin, and on the outside
a log one at that, gleaming with varnish and with yellow
trim for the framings of which naturally no inch may
ever fade, flake or peel. No conspicuous consumption.
The lawn chairs that do get brought out though rarely sat
in are of supermarket quality, hardly a dollar apiece better than ours; dinners one imagines are TV, to save time
for more tidying inside; and the car-park or whatever
such areas are called in the thickly settled parts of suburbs
where they are indigenous and necessary, although mind-
boggling in these surroundings cannot have cost much
besides effort to make. Four cars can be there if the front
two don't have to be gotten out and if all are perfectly
aligned, but any deviation from a right angle would be an
affront anyway. A pipe railing painted white defines the
limit of this quite terrifying space, positively shrieking its
call to conformity to the last sixteenth of an inch, and no
Aubusson carpet ever got more constant and devoted
care than its gravel flooring, destined it's true to be dese-
crated by tires and vicissitudes of weather but that only
calls out the owners' best. A pebble on the lawn? Good

Lord how horrible, how could it happen, why wasn't I
told before? But that's imaginary; there never has been
one. As to the four cars, that's rare, one extra seems to be
the proper limit for cleaning up after, but any guests who
come are most likely relatives, willing to join the work
force; perhaps the mania runs in the family. At any rate
when the figures to be seen number a few more than the
usual, the strays are always behaving exactly like their
hosts, plodding around with clippers and skimmers and
suds and trash baskets and rakes and of course the two
lawn-mowers, at most for ten minutes in exhaustion at the
end of a day reclining in one of those web-and-aluminum
lawn chairs, staring glumly at a pool in desperate need of
having its reflections swept out. It is not, for a wonder, a
suburban concrete pool, but a big one excavated and fed
from a brook like ours, so the problem is acute. With the
flood this summer it became a great deal worse than that,
and there may have been some heart attacks as a result,
but what I'm interested in is something more in the regular run of things, and I wish Tiresias or any other qualified
seer could give me some pointers on it.

There is a palpable sense of attraction in passing the
house of the Tidies, whether they happen to be there or
not. People are known to have disappeared in the vicinity,
either permanently or to return with a strange reticence
forever after about their adventure; beagles and other
hunting dogs who get lost nearby, as they frequently do,
if they turn up at last are never the same again, psycholog-
ically; something haunts them, they keep turning to smell
behind them, as though confusing their masters with their
prey. Now I have no reason to think the family in question are not, on one level, decent God-fearing Republi-
cans holding down respectable and even reasonably

honest jobs, say in insurance or electronics. If each one singly should be hell to have around an office that's not my affair; they wouldn't own it, there'd be a limit to their influence and how many other people's desks and files they would dare to tidy up. Here it's a different story— oh very different: everybody for miles around is affected. Visitors coming to see us for the first time never fail to comment on the experience, and noting our slovenly ways as they wouldn't have otherwise, they wonder at our immunity. I do myself.

We all know obsessions are catching. The first lemming who left home to head for the sea was probably considered a kook, and then look how it ended up. I do not honestly believe, now in the 20th Century A.D., that the Tidies are snatching wayfarers out of their cars and turning them into self-propelled brooms and hedge-clippers, though they may have had forebears who did. I doubt if even a beagle has come to such an end there. But this I must say. It takes a stout heart to drive by that scene without wanting, actually *wanting*, to stop and offer to help. When you see people sacrificing everything else in life to engage in unequal, not to say hopeless combat against the disorder of the universe, the sense of your own inferiority becomes overwhelming and anything seems better than wallowing in it another minute. There's a practical consideration too. With the idea of untidiness made so ghastly and vivid, like the future punishment of the wicked in the Jonathan Edwards sermon referred to earlier, not only do your own sins in that respect loom and grow; inanimate objects begin developing a volition of their own to make it all worse. The zipper on your jeans won't stay shut; your frayed sneaker-laces break; your address book rears up and spills its pages all over the floor;

the leaf-muck at the bottom of your pond turns black, obviously from the intrusion of something like a Loch Ness monster. For half an hour you rush about scouring and sorting, to no avail; it only makes you more mindful of what's undone—and if all that were done there would still be the stars in heaven to straighten out. Nearer at hand, one of the worst times was when the Tidies had been in residence for a full ten days, on what I suppose they called a vacation; one or another of us has to drive by every day to go for the mail, and although we determined long ago to keep silence and a stiff upper lip, if necessary lashing ourselves to the steering wheel, the result was that our septic system broke down, or broke open, anyway became deficient and intolerable. There had never been anything wrong with it before; there was no other possible explanation than the influence of the Tidies, and it cost us a pretty penny. Even so there'd be that tug as you went by; the messier things got at home the more you felt it.

But now I feel sorry for them, and some day when the cobwebs are thick and the weeds high and the will falters I may even go so far as to miss them. They did keep us all on our toes, I have to admit it; still do, only there's a For Sale sign, tidily lined up with the parking rectangle, and the grounds out of habit or terror must have barbered themselves in recent weeks. Everything is spick-and-span as always, but nobody has been visible there since the week after the flood, when as soon as the road was open they arrived and saw their labor of years, the very substance of their lives, turned to a cruel joke. It was one of the worst spots in the neighborhood. The road had caved in smack at their property line; the stream gone berserk like Ares on the battlefield sent their pretty pond swirling all over the landscape, to subside a dismal slough not even cattle would have waded in, the lawn had vanished under rocks enough for a Maine beach.

Somehow, and the thought defies imagination, they tidied up, and then fled, apparently forever, beaten at last. I wonder though if whoever buys the place won't be of the same kind, or become that way after spending a night or two in the house. Something tells me they'll be pretty prompt about rolling up their sleeping bags and washing and putting away their dishes in the morning before scampering for the outdoor tools. Certain influences are very hard to kill, in fact for all I know the Tidies themselves may have been as sloppy as the rest of us before they started weekending on that particular piece of land.

Rain, heavy—speaking of dismal; it's that and then some—to deflect regret at leaving, if one believed in such purpose. You wouldn't have to be exactly an egomaniac —lots of people packing up and leaving summer places right now—only the kind of maniac that gets swept to the fore, and to the mike and platform, in political campaigns: the "our kind" or "our team" varieties. Psychoanalysis must have a term for it.

Three most touching characters in Odysseus' visit to the edge of the underworld—wonderful passage in general though one brings to it too much later reverberation from Virgil and Dante. But then there's nothing in Homer that isn't orchestrated that way, to enormity, to the very limits of memory and understanding. Personal memory far from omitted, though very far from all. Scenes of childhood are one instrument: a room or chair

in a room, where first I trembled at Scylla and Charybdis;
a schoolroom or walk in street or field with a friend years
later marked by discovery of what and where they are.
But couldn't have known then—and perhaps still can't
now—why Odysseus had to sail between them at such
awful cost, and how Homer could make it matter so
much and so long, down to this minute and beyond, that
he did and did have to.

One: his mother, who died, she says, of no disease but
missing him, and now must turn to vapor in his arms.

Two: Ajax, who will not forgive. Something that happened after the end of the Iliad; Achilles' mother, sea-
nymph Thetis, putting up his armor (the set we saw
Hephaestus making, or the earlier, lent to Patroclus and
which A. must have recaptured when he killed Hector?)
as prize in the funeral games. Odysseus won, over Ajax,
that's explicit, but by guile? unfairly? Sorry, I'm only
half-remembering this story—it's not in Homer; where,
how, how long ago did I hear or read it, where do we get
it from? Must be from one or some of the many other
Trojan War stories, put together maybe in Alexandria,
that Homer left out. Well, considering that he didn't even
bother with the Trojan horse we all grew up on or the
end of the war (just a couple of passing refs. to the
horse) ... We see Odysseus wishing he hadn't won, anyhow, and something else I'm hazy about—vile ignorance,
bad dog, down!—Ajax dying "by his own hand." But
wait, that comes back to me—why of course, it was terrible to be defeated in those games, nothing like our Olympic trials and tribulations. God-given prowess, honor
supreme was at stake; it was several hundred years after
Homer, I believe, that bright Greeks began spurning

them and separating spiritual from physical excellence. So poor Ajax, whom Homer never calls dim-witted—Shakespeare got that too from the Alexandrian or some other bundle—was so humiliated he lost his mind and went out and killed a flock of sheep, thinking they were enemies. Then our old friend Mrs. Fixit Athena, that busybody—wisdom indeed! but yes, it does sometimes get overbearing even just in cap and gown, even without deriving from Nature as we're told she did—restores his wits, hence twofold humiliation, so he kills himself, I forget how but with his sword I suppose. Humiliated heroes didn't jump out windows or hang themselves in those days. This is awful, but his turning away from Odysseus, refusing their old bond, is more heartbreaking, we had seen them in such brave comradeship.

Three: the boy Elpenor, a nondescript young crew member, nothing to brag about, run-of-the-mill puller at the oar but likable, who got drunk and fell off the roof as they were leaving Circe's house, for the roundabout and tormented route home to Ithaca—home that dreamlike gets farther, not nearer, with nearly every effort and adventure. The boy begs for decent burial, by fire, and rather oddly, considering all the other crew members who have been lost in various dreadful ways, they will do it, going back to Circe's house to get the body. Of course they couldn't have given burial to a shipmate who'd been eaten alive by the Cyclops or lost overboard; it's just that after so much loss and hardship, their caring enough to bother about one uninteresting youth is startling. Reverence—combined with the matey sort of heartfelt loyalty, the real grief Homer conveys in every loss—had not been driven out of them. They remain phenomenal in quality of heart, Odysseus most for all his brains, but the rest too, yet of a foolishness that is about to cost all but the leader their lives.

Sex very easy-going, quite refreshing in lack of detail or emphasis for these days. O. gets around the worst witches by going to bed with them.

There's an Elpenor here, gets drunk at times though not a patch on his father and hasn't broken his neck yet. Odd jobs; ski patrol—he's good enough for that and it's a plus with girls; runs back-hoe, payloader etc. with pleasant periods loafing on Unemployment. No real swagger, just pretty sure of himself around home here, with the appropriate degree of swagger for that, and was absolutely terrified on a weekend in Boston though in a private apartment; like most local young people he's made friends in the ALS set, and a couple had taken him along on a visit to relatives. Stayed at the TV in the apartment all weekend, scared to go out alone, the others having things to do. But what's special about this boy is a certain real kindness, goodness of heart that there's not much outlet for. The two crippled old widows, mother and daughter, who live near his family's ex-farm, on the backest of back roads, speak of him as practically a saint, he's so good to them, and couldn't care less that school after ninth grade was not where he chose or would ever have consented to be. They don't know what they'd do without him, shoveling snow, chopping wood, bringing mail and groceries. It's all for no pay of course and he managed to do some of it even when he wasn't living at home but several miles away, shacked up with one of the blond N.Y. swingers working at the central ski lodge. There's no question a lot of people would go out of their way, even through storms and over bad roads if necessary, to

give him a decent burial, if he'd been killed in a car crash
or missed his footing on the top rung of a ladder when
hung over like that other poor shade he never heard of,
three-thousand-odd years ago.

Then another tantalizing piece of story-telling—
though when you've just seen Tantalus himself forever
up to his neck in the pool that turns to fire at the touch
of his lips while he forever dies, if the dead could die, of
thirst—really the word won't do. Call this stroke of
Homer's artful, brilliant, fascinating, and deeply disturb-
ing in the manner of the best ghost stories. The unex-
plained, the merely adumbrated lingers long after, to tease
and perplex. The end of the great wanderer's story we'll
hear ages later, from Dante—a version of it, said to be of
uncertain origin, perhaps an invention of the Middle
Ages. Homer is not going to tell it. His listeners surely
knew it, and he, greatest of all story-tellers, knew the most
difficult secret of his craft: when enough is enough. So he
throws it out, light as a handkerchief, portentous as any
Delphic utterance, from the mouth of Tiresias, quite a
few episodes and years before the scene when he does
choose to put down his harp and be led silent from the
megaron. Many must have called "Tell more, tell more!"
but if he did we don't know it. We must puzzle out for
ourselves the true nature of these wanderings and of the
wanderer, and of his bitter tears of longing, after seven
years of amorous dalliance with Calypso, for the home in
Ithaca that only pretends to be the end. We know that his
death will be "sea-borne," which seems to mean not by
shipwreck but from some enemy arriving by sea—in one
version, his own son by Circe; he will have family and
friends around him, so dies at home or much closer to it
than the Middle Ages chose to imagine, but still hardly in

tranquillity. And this follows a still more cryptic announcement of the mysterious challenge he must face in some inland territory, in itself one presumes disquieting to the island man and seafarer—to dispel Poseidon's anger? There had to be some such logic to it, to be felt well enough without elucidation, and nothing could tell us more clearly that he has not been without fault; something there is, beyond pride of intellect, related surely to the unforgivable injury to Ajax, that must be expiated. All his yearnings for hearth and bed in Ithaca, like faces of crystal flash and turn in the mind through these facts and the splendor of reticence about them.

At lunch in Saratoga yesterday an old acquaintance said eagerly yes, how great it would be to hear Homer aloud, "on the radio, for instance," and I was abashed at our luck for over three months hearing it as we have. Not just one person to another either, often five or six or more, each one's voice and laughter or whatever response—and how strong and ready they can't help being—becoming integral to the story as they should be. Yes, radio or records would be something, and are what the life-means of most of us could afford. We too have no such luxury to take for granted, nor the dazzling extra one of starting it in May in Crete, evenings before going out for dinner, over one of the most graceful of harbors; fresh too from Agamemnon's home and several others deprived of their men for ten years by Helen's silliness. It does make a great difference, in what we see in sculpture too, being or having been where it happened and belongs. The Elgin marbles in London are educational; fortunately no computer can tell how diminished they are by their exile or might have been by other forces without it.

Lucky, lucky; all very well to say . . . Yet I do know

it, and bless and love it, this luck of mine, of ours. And have KOFU'd, a modest accomplishment.

In the marvelous brightness again today the pool has started receding toward its winter secrets, three months before the triple-decker mystery: snow as white as birch-bark is now in this light, coal-black I imagine hidden below, the layer of ice in fancy fluctuations between. It's the black that shows suddenly now, a curious develop-ment, after the various sorghum shades of summer. Black and red it is, giving notice overnight—time's up! school's open, too cold to swim, don't need you any more. The gamut of reds, with some gold splashes, cast from the height across the brook look more stylish as reflections in that deepening black than up where they actually are.

Where do the salamanders go? What happens to the bullfrogs?

The wild geese flying over. Cars rushing by, more every time we come back, so many new houses up the road. God help us—sometimes I almost understand those three words. Almighty Zeus, give us favorable winds. I cried again, once, waking in the middle of the night. Frustration at every turn, all day, everything just too impossible. Always loved fall best and thought this one would destroy me, whatever that might mean. Destroy will, spirit, I suppose, curiosity. Become a lump, make meaningless gestures and sounds with the vocal cords, wait for the end. Is that it? Many do. Oh yes I was spoiled all summer and how well I knew it and the reshuffle it would cost later. But minded most what I hadn't foreseen —a moment's positive pride, almost pleasure, in overcom-

ing the handicap in some trivial regard. Gee, look at me,
I'm not so helpless after all. Psychologists say that's the
healthy attitude, what all the mental-health pros preach
and try to inculcate, and I say to hell with them. That's
the one moment I despise myself for. If I need lies to cheer
me, I'll take gloom. Affliction—any loss of faculties or
what gave life sense—is abominable; admit it; wail, rail,
shake your fist—that's what I call healthy.

Indefinitely? You want to go on raging like that for
maybe twenty-some years?

No.

Well then. You said a while back you didn't want to get
used to it.

Certainly not. Categorically.

So you reject the only three alternatives. 1) Get used to
it, meaning resigned, maybe just forgetting part of every
day how different your expectations once were. 2) Be
cheerful, think of the good blah blah blah as per therapy
manual (I guess, have never seen one). 3) Keep raging. Of
course there's a fourth, blowing your brains out, but you
don't seem to be considering that for some reason. Do you
mean to say that if you didn't love your family or have
one, you'd think some gup about the human race in its
ruinous proliferation was sufficient argument against suicide?

Don't be ridiculous. Anybody who's against birth control and abortion has to be a criminal idiot. Still, I'm
evidently a child willy-nilly of the Greco-Roman-Chris-
tian tradition, along with any other of similar parti pris.
Once the child is born, life is supposed to be let's say
secularly sacred; certainly there's peril to more than the
principals in doing away with it. Suicide and murder both

do leave a stench, you know, like one of those gases escaping from certain chemical plants.

And if the life in question is a hopeless mess?

Hard to judge. Can you see all the ripples out from your acts good or bad? But lay off, I'm no rockbottom-dogmatist. Not just Socrates; plenty of other cases noble or sensible, or where it would have been better.

Your godmother, the last years?

Ah . . . But I loved her, you know.

(Rude laugh.) And if you hadn't existed?

(Long pause.) No. I'm glad she didn't do that. Or think of it. Decent people didn't in her day. Of course some expert, in some discipline or other, would say exactly, just the result of her upbringing in a rather stable, prosperous and sentimental period of society, and the ruthless customs of certain primitive peoples would make more sense now. Leaving out small rural places, who do you know down the street anyway? so junk the human-bond bit, give to the United or whatever Fund for conscience' sake and make it the accepted and expected thing for the old and otherwise useless to get rid of themselves. I wonder what word to give to what would then be missing. Fortitude, charity—old hat, who'd understand? Nevertheless as to my godmother's last years, if I hadn't existed I say she would still have put a penny in the pot without which we'd be poorer than foxes. Have you ever happened to notice what's strewn around the mouth of a fox-den?

But look, those alternatives—there isn't just a front door; there may be several, plus windows, and cracks here and there too. The girl I mentioned can boast of all that and what's more a dog-door, the plastic fan type, through which she has sometimes had to reach for the lock bur-

glar-fashion, with hooked wires etc. when the key had
been left inside. Faced by thorny questions, as by lack of
a key, she is adept at the bypass and the Approach Circui-
tous.

In this instance, returning as usual in September to a
Connecticut house left immaculate by model summer tenants, she was, I won't say saved but spun around, brought
up short by 1) the chicanery of repairmen, and 2) the
sufferings of friends. Cancer mostly, and no regard for
age or income. We've cleared the decks pretty much of
TB, smallpox, polio to make way for this, and now medical research comes, or in recent years did come, under the
term of abhorrence in Washington—*programs.* It would
take funds, and brains, and education to furnish the brains.
Out of taxpayers' money! unthinkable. They'd rather
take their chances, it's a lottery, not everybody gets hit,
some still die of old age. So build up the "private sector"
instead and everything will be hunky-dory; and by all
means let's hurry up and discover some kind of life on
Mars. The young poet I was talking about still wants to
go and will leave an interesting record buried under a
chunk of lava. As I intimated, he's one of those who are
rather tired of the way things are going on the home
planet, silly boy.

Another angle on the private sector (used to be called
business) comes in with the repairmen. I said they did a
lot to restore my shattered spirits and so they did, by the
technique of the counter-irritant. Nothing like a good fit
of specific frustration and fury for chasing out the amor-
phous kind, or doldrums. In the presence of a General
Westix serviceman a doldrum cannot survive; it shrivels,
utterly defeated. I say GW only to single out one from
the twenty-six similar incidents of the same week. Any

other would do as well, involving a bent car-fender, leak-ing boiler, malfunctioning thermostat, racking cough in washing machine, sulking vacuum cleaner that will only exhale, a fire and burglar alarm system that brought the police cars Monday when a fly crossed its line of vision and stayed mum as a clam Tuesday for half a kitchen in flames (no burglars that week) etc. Never mind the dehumidifier that has turned itself into a sprinkler or the mystery well that appeared in the cellar, the work of some peevish nymph I believe; at least I distinctly heard a female voice from there telling us to get out of our own house if we didn't like it. Like it? We love it! We've spent twenty-four years and sweat of our brows by the bucket-ful molding it to our hearts' desire. I just wish I had a degree from M.I.T. and the grey-eyed goddess Athena a little more on my side.

It was just the clock on the stove I wanted fixed, be-cause the way things are now it's the only one in the house I can tell time by. Clock, I said to the woman on the GW phone; nothing else, don't want the timer, never have used it, only have it because I couldn't get the stove without it even though it cost extra. So now I said again very clearly just clock. She said minimum charge $14.95. I said that's a lot for a kitchen clock, I could get one for $7.50 —that was a few days ago, they're $9.95 now—but I need it so all right. The main or perhaps only qualification for suburban servicemen is being tall and personable; there must be sidelines to the job that I wouldn't know about. The tall personable young man strode haughtily to the kitchen, miffed from the start to find a housewife, in bathrobe all right—it was 8:20 A.M.—but considerably over thirty. He pulled the stove out two inches, gave it a poke on the upper rear, pushed it back and said, "We don't repair clocks. We only replace the whole timer unit. $71." I repressed the relevant piece of my mind and said the voice on the GW telephone should have told me that. He got a bit more sourpussed and made out a bill for $19.95. I said he'd been in the house exactly ninety seconds and done nothing and if that wasn't minimal I didn't know what was, anyhow I wasn't going to pay ten cents still less any $19.95 or $14.95 when they had no business sending him in the first place. He said would I sign the invoice. I said no. Am still waiting for an upper-echelon voice to call back as promised. Of course we'll get the bill for $19.95 anyway but I just want to ask a few personal questions, like the name of the president of the corp. and what ski-lifts does he patronize.

Still, that's nothing to body-repair shops and their recondite arrangements with insurance companies. There's a Polyphemus for you; get in that cave and they'll have you for dinner. Wednesday for a few minutes I considered a version of the Odysseus ruse. While they were inside adding on another $100 I would slip under the car, give it a push and with agility born of desperation, like the mariners under the one-eyed giant's sheep, hang on to the axle for dear life while the car rolled down the hill, away from that robbers' den. But they must have suspected something and came out too soon.

By Thursday so much else of the same sort had happened, and the bank account was so depleted, I was just glad to be alive; which was the point of this narrative. A miracle, you might say. Something does move in mysterious ways its wonders to perform, and logical positivism or negativism to circumvent. The cat came back too, a matter for rejoicing. I had searched hours along the road, having suffered too many griefs from it even in earlier years, when it was nothing like now.

I was all wrong about "dree." Education, lovely goddess, where have you been hiding from me? Oh seasons of longing, oh castles of regret! It means "to suffer," "to endure," transitive. So the cat and I, dreeing our weirds in the cabin that day of terrible rain before the flood, were not counting or reciting anything but just putting up with our fates as best we could.

Labor Day weekend item from this vicinity, or Boys Will Be Boys. A group of young teen-agers, of the usual "good" middle-class families we hear, stole a prize calf, killed and ate it, whether or not in some cultist rite, and in the course of the barbecue one member of the expedition was stabbed to death. The drug-den in our back field, in the little pine grove we planted many years ago, seems to have gone out of use for some reason. The boys we caught doping there last spring were older, at least eighteen; not to be accused of sex discrimination must assume there were girls too on other occasions. The picnic bunch had probably never seen a live calf before outside our county livestock museum so you can't blame them for getting a little overexcited.

A lot of talk about "justice" in such connections—not social but legal justice, seems to have grown big as a topic. A stunning event bearing on it, not that Homer quite puts it that way, is what befell the fine Phaeacian ship and crew that at last, after the approximately twenty years of mishaps at sea and war before, put Odysseus ashore on his beloved island of Ithaca, along with a great treasure in gifts from the royal house and peers of that hospitable little realm. The king's kindness and courtesy have been brilliantly timed; one other fright or setback just then would have been one too many. So we get instead the shock of an orderly and gentle place, conviviality, promise of safe passage home, everything pleasant—except that the poor princess Nausicaa who was responsible for the happy outcome is probably pining away upstairs for love of the gorgeous hero and doesn't get mentioned again; and except for the one surly fellow who taunts Odysseus with gratuitous insults into showing his prowess at the games in his honor. A nice touch, to avoid the saccharine and remind us we're dealing with real people, and he is made to apologize afterwards. And story-telling—a feast and marvel of it, along with plenty of food and wine of course. The stories come from the blind bard with harp —a self-portrait, or possible source of the idea that Homer was blind? must try to find out what the scholars say—and Odysseus himself, telling a good part of his adventures to those enthralled listeners. I wonder if narrative in all literature was ever so brilliantly framed. I can't think of any to put beside it or anywhere near it. Boccaccio and Chaucer not comparable at all; those are bundles of disparate tales, arbitrary bouquets. This work draws slowly in like a giant fishnet, all of a piece, every part working for the same suspense and with such cunning in the circling. Way back we had Odysseus naked and alone fighting waves and exhaustion to reach that shore, and all the excitements of his story are enclosed in the suspense over his leaving it; way back too we left Penelope in one danger, Telemachus in another, and never stop waiting for those outcomes either, no matter how well we know them.

The justice incident—well, there are many, and you might say both the Iliad and the Odyssey are mainly on that theme—but the particular example, concerning that boat and crew, is so strange to our minds it's quite hard to imagine it was ever thought of otherwise, granted all the acceptance of caprice on the part of the gods. Which amounts to saying caprice by life, fate being no rewarder of virtue, even if society may sometimes punish the wicked. But this is carrying the notion rather far, and as if furthermore there were some kind of rightness, of a moral order, about it. The sailors, all tops in honor as in physical fitness apparently, must have broken their backs in the feat of nightlong rowing at top speed, while Odysseus sleeps on the splendid couch set up for him on deck —not that we know exactly what the deck consisted of, but that's another question. They laid him dutifully on the beach at Ithaca, still asleep, with the treasure beside him, and without a moment's rest pulled off for home. Poseidon, furious with Odysseus for blinding his horrid son Polyphemus, complains to Zeus and gets from him the curious suggestion that instead of pursuing our hero any farther, he take it out on the Phaeacian crew, and through them the whole generous and innocent kingdom. But not innocent toward him, Poseidon—there's the rub, though why he should be allowed any sympathy or rage in connection with such a son as Polyphemus it must have been hard even for a contemporary Greek to grasp. Zeus however has to avoid war in heaven as far as possible, even if he enjoys a good scrap up there at times, so Poseidon by way of compromise turns boat and crew, returning from their noble mission and in sight of home port, to stone; and there they have remained ever since.

Deep, isn't it? Yes. Come back to it some time.

Prodge back in college three weeks now, Ennie off to France yesterday. No killing frost yet, flowers usually poor from our absence but this time it's all a Bonnard, wild color-mixes, glorious. We dig in. Our very dear friend Yuri, eighty, is dying, and the hospital won't let him do it peacefully. Has been in agony for days.

Violent ambivalence toward all my new toys—and the next time I hear the word "aids" I intend to misbehave. Paraplegics can't like it much either, at least the first year or two. Salesmen's word, and I wish all my friends so lucrative a business. House strewn with these new objects, big, little, black, white, portable, importable. Great fish-eyes leering up from beside bed or telephone, or bending from spring-controlled neck at end of metal tendril rooted in weighted base on the floor, announcing it's there to stay, once and for all. Baby googlies giggling at bottom of purse, crawling around bureau drawers, liable to turn up asleep in a glove or anywhere. Big Momma loosens a spring, leans toward your armchair, turning on monstrous illumination like smile of hired sympathy: "How's it going today, Lovey? And what a lovely day it is! Well, here I am to help you, now let's see . . ." Shit. Knock it over if you could. No, costs too much. Just ignore its personality, try to use it, and remember you were showing off all these things with a certain childish pride to a visitor only yesterday.

Bad piece of timing by the darling doctor in this matter, his only mistake as far as I know. He brought it up too soon. I wasn't ready, family either, tears theirs that time; one had misunderstood on the previous visit, thought there was hope. I knew better but even so when I heard him sending me to Dr. Zero the bottom fell out. On Dr. Z.'s door the sign reads, "Lasciate ogni speranza voi ch'entrate"; somebody has pasted two or three Happy stickers around it, grin-line in stupid circle-face, revolting product of current national schmaltz. Philosopher friend was right. Some truths better not told, at least not without subtle preparation and few are born that subtle. The d.d. should have lied a little, said "Maybe eventually, not certain, we'll see . . ."

So eventually got through Dr. Z.'s door, more dead than alive; others in same or worse condition in waiting-room, some very young. Breezy fellow—dept. store Santa Claus, cajole the kiddies, get them smiling like the stickers on the door, which maybe he put up himself. And little by little acquired the hateful things, when the rest of me wasn't looking, and more hatefully could sometimes reach for them without hate, as people do with an ordinary pair of glasses. Thus is custom established and rebellion gnawed away, exactly as under political dictatorship.

That was going on all summer but no occasion then for other angers and self-denigration that arise now, on any foray into the city. The saleslady, the girl at the cafeteria counter treat you like an idiot, so you feel like one. The affliction apparently doesn't show, or not enough; the sign, arrow, price-tag, cottage cheese versus fruit salad are right under your nose; naturally you cringe before these people, when not wanting to beat the bejeesus out of them instead. But look who's complaining at their rudeness and unkindness. You wouldn't want to exchange your life and mind for theirs, would you? you think they have no grievances of their own? As to the pariah bit, it would be worse in Latin countries. Cripples, any physical defect or deformity bad luck, avoided like plague; no mercy; can't afford it. Something to be said for that, at least sanctioned by ancient superstition as against our offhand meanness; you'd know where you stood.

Better perhaps to be needing cane and seeing-eye dog? No, muggers go for that; the cafeteria worker would be still nastier. "They ought to go eat someplace else, not come here bothering us, right at the worst lunch hour too. They got their own places to go to, people like that." Have they? where? what kind of places? New stage. New influx of Others. Pretty soon might be allowed in the front door of the club.

This Is Your Hell. Keep It Happy.

For another grinning circle the summer didn't include we move to an undersea setting. This one is called the Foggy Snorkel. Go into crowded room, many well-known, even good friends, all weeds and corals now until a few inches away, rather pretty. "What's she gotten so uppity about?" Do you hear it or just think you do? Can't go around explaining. If all there were to go on about their ailments—! One woman is doing so. Ex-beauty, ex-wit, ex-excellent company; years of tranquilizers have caught up with her, at fifty a wreck, obsessed with misdeeds of doctors, wrong diagnoses; can't keep her mind more than forty seconds on any topic of general interest; smile over-stretched in panic, about to burst, eyes too, from excess voltage. People murmur sympathy, edge away. If she had the nerve she would be up on a chair, a soapbox, addressing the whole gathering. "Am I dying? is that it?"—scrawny as she has become, hideous with levity. "But I don't know how, I'm not ready, I never learned anything like that! Is my husband already looking around for somebody else to marry? He's so handsome, and brilliant, he wouldn't have any trouble. Does anybody care? Am I boring you?"

She is probably not under mortal sentence for the moment but several are who must be there among the shifting fronds, and you long to speak to them, about that if they chose, or about nothing in particular. You radiate affectionate warmth on a high-gloss thin-brained male stranger, much as a mallet might come down on a box of peanut brittle. Both smiles crumble loudly; an animosity is born. "Oh excuse me, I thought you were . . ." Then a worse kind of mistake, just from too much swimming, or fear of morays among the rocks. You ask Doris, a foot away and familiar for years, if Joe is there too. "Joe?" She decomposes; no candy here; the result this time is more like overcooked hominy, as in view of long mutual esteem she seems willing to assume any features that might fill the bill. She not only isn't and doesn't much resemble Doris; they don't even like each other. She is and always has been Sophie, as you knew perfectly well except for that slip of the brain, and her husband is your old skiing companion, Bob; she also has a son you know well named John; perhaps you meant him? "No, no . . ." You smile sheepishly and flee, promising to explain some other time, which of course you won't, even if the subtle rift doesn't grow to permanent crevasse.

So you've turned into a liar too, and these aren't white lies. They're more the brownish orange of a half-withered tangerine.

Come to think of it though, Doris and Sophie do have a good deal in common. Same age and height more or less, both daughters of well-known musicians, had similar marital difficulties at one time. It was a natural enough mistake, wasn't it? Wasn't it?

Chill rain, hard all day, the kind that always beats down everything but the chrysanthemums. I rush out and rescue all I can of the others, to take to Yuri's funeral. Seashores were his love and theme and it would be good to think of his ashes scattered by one, maybe Normandy or Brittany. But his gentle wisdom was too deep for such histrionics. If anybody wants to, OK, let them; he wouldn't care. A foreigner in much of life, from lies of any kind being so alien to him, he was a native in the deep places of kindness and love. No fuss and feathers about his being at the party or his leaving it. He was here. He's gone. Mourning sets in like a change of wind in the night.

Biked to our nearest store-cluster—no supermarket, can't call it a shopping center yet, praise be—seven miles round trip and never realized before how much more uphill coming back. Scary from cars and air fouled by them, a smack at the lungs each time, but all very pretty just the same; felt good. Then coming home after taking E. to her ship, passed cop-cars, small crowd and ambulance on a back road near here. A boy about ten hit biking, unconscious, a white canopy rigged up over him, as signal to further traffic apparently. Couldn't tell if he was dead.

Stayed up too late several nights, the end of the Odyssey had us so enthralled. Was speaking of it yesterday walking in the back fields with our very literate friend M. and the cocker—the same who got us in trouble on the Long Trail, still frisky but blind now, through his own foolishness, not old age and I hope not out of family solidarity. M. had forgotten that Helen appeared in that volume and that Telemachus did before the end. I can't remember now what I'd forgotten myself. Much more than that I'm sure. I certainly had forgotten how much of the story is told by Odysseus himself, and that he stayed seven whole years with Calypso, and Nausicaa's being so dropped (memory, that joker, must have slipped in a suggestion from Dido and Aeneas, out of geographical association: images of ancient ships and loves of heroes in that part of the Mediterranean) and more shockingly, what a fully given and moving character the swineherd is. Most crucial, hadn't remembered how marvelously pulled out the suspense is, from O.'s arrival in his beggar's disguise at the swineherd's door to the scalp-prickling moment of his picking up the great bow and bending it "effortlessly."

A good deal of slapstick by Athena in there, and some touches that do put Homer, whoever and whatever he was, rather out of it; where you lose the sense of single artistry and remember it had to be true there were many tales to sort among, many versions, at this point or that several kinds of mind pulling it all together. Jaeger *(Paideia)* puts it more strenuously than that and would have the Iliad as we know it date from a very long time after the Odyssey. Well, arguing with scholars is a dog's job and he may be right. From the feel of it all—tricks of narrative technique, spacing of moods, variations in pace etc.—it would seem the great difference between the two works was well enough accounted for by the extreme difference in subject matter. When you're dealing with war then you're dealing with warlike things and attributes, and the view of "later" peacetime aristocratic life we're told we get in the Odyssey takes up very few pages, most of them about the Phaeacians. They were not warlike, but Knossus long before any possible Homer or Iliad had no reason to be fortified either, so we're told and so the ruins indicate.

Which brings us back to the curious chastisement of those pleasant people, after their kindness to our hero. Injustice we call that sort of thing, with *rank* (adj.) before it. Their king, Alcinous, doesn't take it that way. He says that a seer long ago foretold the event, and its clear lesson is that now they must stop being so hospitable and giving free passage to strangers from their shores. Mysterious reasoning to our minds but presumably not to a Greek's any time in the eight-hundred-odd-year period from Troy to Plato. There seems—this is just horse sense and guesswork—to lie in the king's conclusion a strong hint of wars and social changes to come, and advice to toughen up in preparation for them. Zeus is arbitrary in plenty of details but does "view the wide world" and therefore has to weigh some pretty long-term values with every nod and thunderbolt; the Greeks were far too intelligent to go on pouring out wine and burning choice hunks of fat for him if he hadn't. Although Odysseus, once the slaughter of the suitors is accomplished and the mess washed up, will have come home at last to peace, that is just the end of his particular tale of wanderings; also, along with the glimpse of Helen back home with Menelaus and old Nestor comfortable in his palace at Pylos instead of clanging around and camping however luxuriously on a beach far away, it is the end of the Trojan War. But not of wars, not of wickedness either, and perhaps Poseidon's petulance and Zeus's go-ahead on it have a deeper wisdom than what we would consider just, warning the Phaeacians that the time for their gentle courtesy has come to an end.

Not the last time the sacred notion of hospitality would

come to grief. We were told last spring that back in the
beautiful mountains of Crete the farmers and villagers still
hold that religious view of welcome to the stranger and
until quite lately acted on it. It began to be abused, as the
Long Trail shelters were, and by the same kind of people,
many of them young Americans. The word got out, free
food and lodging up there, and more. The idle guests,
received at first, even after World War II, with ancient
honor, not only settled in on their usually poor and always hard-working hosts; they stole from them, plun-
dered them, until now people are having to lock their
doors and call to any stranger No! go away! and this has
caused them great suffering, the old idea they and their
ancestors grew up with was so powerful.

Guests of that stripe, the suitors, get what's coming to
them in Odysseus' house, and that's one slaughter it's impossible to feel anything but pleased about. We can't wait
for the arrows to hit their marks, and the spears when the
arrows are used up, even if it's a bit unsporting, typically
so, of Athena to deflect all the suitors' weapons; however,
it was four men against eighty or so and O. was absolutely
in the right. You're not allowed to question that and you
don't. Virtue and vice have been too unequivocal though
so humanly flecked, with no stroke of parable; and the
death of the outcast old dog, on recognizing the master
absent twenty years, that Dickensian tear-jerker, has put
you in no mood to pity the young blades who caused him
to be out on the dungheap. But their crime?—that's interesting. Not their wanting to marry the rich supposed
widow, who incidentally must have been at least ten or
fifteen years older than any of them; they are in fact very
decorous in their behavior toward Penelope and only go
to bed with the maids, and of them only the only too

willing, thus showing an aristocratic breeding stronger
than their characters as s.o.b.'s, also keeping Greek Ideal
Womanhood free of any vulgar touches that might linger
in the mind. No, their crime is single and simple, only
highlighted a bit by their being mean to a dog and the
man they take for a beggar. What they are guilty of, and
we are glad to see them die for, is nothing but free-loading, a particularly arrogant form of stealing: gorging
without being invited on another's food and wine.

So off to the underworld with them, and there, without
any stirring of regret over their fate—certainly not, or
that of the bad maids either—we get a few lines that a
millennium or so later could almost have passed for Christian in feeling. They have, not souls—evidently a notion
alien to the Greek mind—but a dim survival in replica.
We're seeing and hearing them there among the shades
while their bodies are still heaped up in the courtyard. It's
a pity, the tone seems to say, that they were so idle and
greedy and insensitive.

You get wondering if the floor of the hall was of wood.
It wasn't. It was earthen and when the few loyal survivors
are cleaning up the blood they do it with hoes. Penelope
won't be permitted to wake up from the bizarre sleep
Athena has cast on her, and see the room and her husband,
until it is all proper and decent again. The archery contest
was to be, and when Odysseus got to it was, apparently
a matter of standing or more likely sitting on a low stool
in the doorway and shooting out. Vase paintings, I'm told,
depict the bow held horizontally. The famous row of
twelve axe-halve sockets that O.'s arrow would go
through had been aligned by Telemachus on a ridge he
quickly made for the purpose in the courtyard. As he had
never seen it done, this was thought quite brilliant on his

part, though one would think any boy in his right mind
could figure it out. It's not considered right for women
to admire male prowess these days, but I wish Penelope
could have seen her husband's arrow whizzing through
that row of little holes, I really do.

   I wonder if being able to see straight lines again
might be, partly at least, a matter of psychological correc-
tion. The retina might still be registering waves and wob-
bles—Samson pulling the columns down, everything just
about to go—but learned from the brain a kind of simulta-
neous translation. Probably not but if true would be fascinating, and then you'd wonder if just the human brain
could do it or if animals could be that smart too. Some
might be more so, with the help of other capacities we
lack. But of course the role of interpretation goes way
beyond any such mechanics, however complex; takes you
into every deep water there is. The cat, who shares my
study in Vermont but never here, has just come in with
a small squeak of announcement, approached for a touch
of corroboration and is now lying watchfully by the
door. She must have known I was puzzling over her cerebral powers. Or may just feel lonely or want lunch.
   The Moose is watchful too. Yes, I still have him in
mind, now and then, for perspective's sake. We're still
trooping through his tent, all the billions of us on our free
family ticket. Only he's grown, not so much physically as
in other ways; I see him differently. He's become a kind
of Zeus-Moose, although passive in appearance, just ob-
serving our fates, not dealing them out. Yet we are
changed by finding ourselves in such a line and will go out

the other side of the tent not quite what we were when
we went in. Occasionally he stamps, or defecates or
chews; the trainer, really his servant, brings him water and
a bale of hay. On Olympus they went in for food and
drink too and plenty of copulation; we don't hear about
the latrine part, or sex details either, any more than for
mortals; the Greeks clearly had an innate aversion to boredom and sense of where it sets in, at the outer edge of the
over-explicit and the vulgar, a main distinction between
them and the Romans. Yet in one physiological regard
Homer is explicit to a nicety, in the Iliad alone. Dozens
of deaths in battle are given with exquisite precision, as to
where the weapon entered the body, what sinew or organ
was ruptured, etc., before mist veils the eyes—one of
those nearly compulsory formulations, like dawn "with
her fingertips of rose" (just rosy-fingered, without the tips
I believe, in previous translations) or the opening of any
address to a person of high degree.

The details of the killings seem odd, among so many
restraints and courtesies, and must partly explain the
rather prevalent dislike of the book in our times, as against
the Odyssey. All right, let's say there's too much of it for
our tastes, but we would scarcely grasp the nature of
hand-to-hand combat without it; the war itself and the
profession of arms would be a blur of platitude and dull
reiteration, since so many deaths do have to be reported.
The physical details, along with frequent references to
family background and grief in store at home, keep interest possible. And listeners in the first few hundred years,
for most of whom war was a fairly constant fact of life,
must have cared extremely about which parts of the body
were less or more vulnerable and to what. Aesthetically,
wounds inflicted are the base, a necessary one given the

subject of the epic, for all the great scenes and themes of another order that make Homer the father of us all—speaking of the non-Oriental, non-underdeveloped part of the world, the only one I can claim much acquaintance with. (Beware the whole hog, in anything.)

Some people would say, or write as if they thought, that sex descriptions should follow the same logic: the more spelled out, the more interest generated. False, except for the handicapped in that domain, the purpose there being to excite and/or titillate, the opposite of Homer's. Death in battle is not something most people experience and we need to visualize it, to understand the characters, but we're not supposed to feel like going out and trying it. Imagination travels out far and instantly from the physical detail in that context. An equivalent treatment of copulation bludgeons it to death in short order, leaving something on the level of toilet habits, also said to be exciting to some morons and sex-cripples.

For real sexiness in literature, Homer is tops—because it's not that, it's sexuality, nothing he had to aim for or stoop to or probably think about as a separate subject at all. It's the grand wind blowing through everything, vast and tricky and assumed like the ever-present sea. It makes and permeates the whole story, via Helen; makes the quarrel between Agamemnon and Achilles that sets off the specific story of the Iliad, through two other bedmates of contention; gives all the pull to Odysseus' homecoming, since if Penelope weren't still waiting for him, and so desperately wishing for him, he and we wouldn't care much if he got there or not. And then that great bit, her trick to test his authenticity and the poet's to ensure rapture in his audience, about the secret construction of their marital bed, just before they will at last go to it together

—now there's something for Madam Imagination to fly off from. Puts his twenty years of other sex-life, occasional or bewitched, in perspective too. Not hers, it's never suggested that she had any, and there could enter the wrangle of the 1970's A.D., but aside from other possible considerations we're talking about a number of centuries B.C., when only goddesses and maidservants could be free in their amours and captive women had no choice.

There are some peculiar touches, even so. Maybe in some other version Menelaus had an impulse to kill Helen, when she had lived nine years as the wife of another man, but in this one he seems content to have her back, no questions asked. Yet when Agamemnon is forced to repent having snatched Achilles' girl, and offers to give her back along with a heap of expensive presents, he makes a big point of never having "lain with her," and evidently you're supposed to believe him or try to. This plainly tells us that she would have been considered damaged goods otherwise. Helen I suppose was undamageable through being half immortal, a daughter of Leda and of all people, Zeus himself. Grandeur takes odd forms, in any era. What is most mystifying in this Greek epic version is that the grand, the heroic—basic ingredient of the genre—goes with such marvelous human subtlety and verisimilitude. From vanities and quirks of any kind to every aspiration and abyss—it's all there and all recognizable. This has probably been said a million times about Homer and is worth saying again, if only because every year brings a new flood of novels nowhere near as much fun to read. Dante, Shakespeare, Tolstoy: really how few there have been who could touch all the strings.

But drop the Great Books course, I only meant to say that Homer——

Has been salvation, speaking personally—is that what I was going to say? I don't know. This is another day. And no, you can't speak of salvation, insane boast, only stages in an evolution: of sorrow, of understanding, of joy in spite of, of simply days passing perhaps though one has to hope for more than that.

Anyhow I'm barely a novice in affliction, as I hope I've known all along and said before. Y.'s death leaves the real thing, sad enough for us his many friends but to Nora, some years younger than he, the massive blow. Her own great heart, guts, brains, character make it so—talent too and dedication to it, all in the same life-package with his. So she sits alone and we have tea as so many times before but this is the first time without him and she is alone in our company or any, though she must fight tiredness and have some and keeps speaking of the goodness of friends, their friends, as if that were not all their creation, out of their goodness. Once we were speaking of a very different, deceptive sort of marriage though also a long one, of people we all knew, and she said, "I can't imagine Yuri and me not trusting each other." He said, "We trust each other because we are trustworthy. X. is not." And have been loved because they were lovable. But how fast and fiercely death goes to work on familiar objects—furniture, rug, paintings, bookshelves, their contents not finished spilling; you could hear it working away like termites as we sipped our tea, and that's what she meant by "I still don't believe it, I keep thinking of things I must remember to tell him." It would be cruel even to think that the onslaught will let up some time, change its pace and method at least, for better or worse.

Carried that suddenly altered and shaken room—more muted rose-color from the carpet than I ever felt it to be

before, so that that seems now far more than black the
color of grief—with us through two big N.Y. bashes:
bangup publisher's cocktail affair for visiting author,
huge public dinner for noble cause. We rarely go to such
things so enjoy them for a change. Saw no particular
ground for satire, except as any large gathering induces
it; saw plenty of demi-friends and admirable achievers of
one sort and another; no horses' asses to speak to though
there must have been a few. Heard a lot about language
capacity in apes and dolphins, and political prisoners in
various foreign countries; a well-known commentator en-
tertained part of the party with jolly platitudes about the
presidential campaign; a drunk at the back of the ball-
room yelled "Yah, yah!" during the speeches. N. had said
they were both reading Proust when he fell ill—the only
piece of uncharacteristic behavior of his life, I can believe,
the illness that is—and now she didn't feel like getting on
with Proust. Or with any highbrow bookfare for a while,
I would think. There are surely times when any little
attention-waster is all that can serve. But if any, it might
be Homer who could reward and not repel the wounded
mind with no comfort of religion to call on. Because he
was not alone in moving so wisely in the depths; in some
sense he must have had all Greeks of quite a few centuries
with him, or they would not have heard him so eagerly
and loved him so long; the same spirit is in the wonderful
friezes at Delphi. So there was no strain in plucking the
deep bass strings, any more than for Bach in composing
for them. The worst that life can do was a knowledge
shared, as we share now a fear of criminals in dark streets,
only that involves only tragedy, not any tragic view of
life. For that you have to have a common aspiration toward all that the Greeks meant by beauty as well.

And from the train window toward midnight saw slum
after slum, dread upon dread hurtling by. No rose room
in immense dignity of grief. No such luck. Life has to be
worth something for mourning to be more than another
beating on frayed nerve-ends, and what young hope,
what gracious old age flowers in those hideous, sinister
streets? It's a long time since we heard of any, or of
anybody saying they loved living there, it was their neighborhood, they felt good walking around in it and never
thought of locking their doors. The new high-rises rear
grotesquely among lots left to trash and weeds, the old-
style tenements falling to ruin whether uninhabited or
still with a light showing through a grimy window or
two, the shut warehouses looking darker than anything
else knows how to be, a field full of crushed cars behind
an incongruous board fence, and locked places for used
body parts—automobile, not human bodies—which in
that passing night-view seem to have assumed with the
end of day a weird and angry voice, cantata style, between a screech and a hum, giving vent to some deep
metallic complaint not permitted to be heard during
working hours. It is the song of the remains of abandoned
cars such as we see all the time alongside the nearby
parkways, carcasses the ants will have been at within
hours or minutes. What's left to be hauled off, when somebody gets around to it, joins in those still, high-crime
hours with the trains' murmurous rattle and the drone of
planes descending through paths tracked by wild geese
for a landing across the bay, in a Mahleresque Song of the
Earth. They sing, for nobody to hear, a memory of
origins inside the planet and of Indian country splendid
with river-views and of Audubon dying among precise
visions of birds not many blocks to the west. Then I

imagine some rusty axle or ball-bearing gets the whole great chorus going in a magnificent tutti, of "Shame! shame! on the species that wastes our substance to create such evil and ugliness, they are not worthy to touch what we are made of, nor are they trustworthy among themselves!" until the Director, possibly from the control tower at J. F. Kennedy, shouts "Again! start again, there was trouble with the tapes, and come in stronger on the 'Shame!'—sound as if you meant it and remember we're on the late, much too late show. Now all together, 'I remember a time . . .' "

What you wouldn't hear down on those streets is a footstep. I remember a time when that was a pleasant and somehow reassuring sound to hear from your bed in New York at night, the sharp tap of women's heels mostly, men's shoes usually more muffled. Only on 125th St. there is stronger light and some sign of life, at least some figures still loitering, for whatever purpose or lack of one. Then we slow up to cross the bridge, and pick up speed again as though being admonished like children to avert our eyes from the awful vista. Most in the train do so naturally, out of habit or weariness; it is the last one of the night that will be more or less full—of suburbanites returning from some kind of evening on the town; some drowse, some chatter, hopped up by novelty or a good or bad time. Like the second hand on a clock the grim streets tick by, the non-residential ones no more in the grip of emptiness and the air of latent panic than those with doors standing for home or at least shelter, beyond sagging stairs or self-service elevators. No difference except the rent; the high-rise is no safer, won't look shiny for long, offers the same desolation to eyes and heart, only perhaps more sense of being defrauded. A lot of windows still lit, a lot of fornication in progress, thousands of TV sets jabbering along watched or not. Not a human figure to be seen. The yellow sodium streetlights are far between, no promise or cheer even for alley cats, with every door bolted as they must be, in those prison-boxes of buildings: called living-quarters, that's how far our language is debased.

You imagine the cat; you feel for him; life is hard. You imagine yourself the criminal—mugger, prostitute, dope-peddler, whatever, perhaps still working downtown at that hour, perhaps with a pad to check in at on one of those streets later on. Another, eerier music, of innumerable cash registers emulating triangles and xylophones, emanates from the mortuary cityscape as we kettledrum by, to get off in alien bunches after a while at our own stations, and so home to our well-fed cat and dog and comfortable bed and thoughts of the ideal of Righteousness on the part of every citizen in the Greek city-state.

Mike F.'s little daughter, we've just heard, has died in the institution.

I notice, with surprise, that I see a good deal better at breakfast-time, not every day but usually. With my fancy light can even read a few lines of newsprint then, laboriously but still; later in the day can't even get headlines. Some days I forget for a minute or two even to be thrilled by it, get interested and read a paragraph as if none of this had happened and force of habit were still operative. Then I remember and have to guard against crazy hope. It comes, you can't help it, it's the secret of Lourdes and what filled me with loathing of that place fourteen years ago; also caused permanent rupture with a devout French Catholic acquaintance we visited the same evening in the country. But didn't you find it beautiful, she asked or rather asseverated, and I said no, I guessed I was too Protestant, I found it quite repulsive. We have never met again, but that might be partly because we gave her little grandson the mumps, unintentionally. I mean we might have done that on purpose if we'd thought of it but we honestly didn't.

Fight this wild breakfast-time joy; you know it's insane; will bring you nothing but worse misery. However, there's a little technical trick connected with it that can be useful, maybe even in a small way remedial. I find if things are quiet in the house—no repairmen at the door, nobody charging through to read the electric meter for an office that's going to overcharge more every week for whatever he tells them: all these angles of life figure—and I deliberately make myself quiet, breathe deeply, shut out annoyances, avoid looking at the clock (new, $12.89, on the wall) I can read the words quite a lot better. A discovery like that would send a good many people to the nearest guru if they weren't hooked that way already and I wouldn't argue with them. TM, just for one such immersion, tends to make people rather passive and boring —neither the infinite nor one's own interior, nor willful vacuum, can be all that absorbing without a price-tag— but otherwise seems harmless enough and may save some people from more offensive habits, like fiddling with matches. I'll just stick with the facts myself, in so far as I can latch on to them.

One of them is the stupid game of Suppose, applying only to afflictions of the body, not the other kinds. A lot of energy and time go into this game, unbeknownst to the

player most often. Many odd moments dribble into it, in
bathtub, between sink and refrigerator, going downstairs
for broom and dustpan when pine needles or grass clip-
pings have been tracked in, moments the head could put
to better use. It would be better if we acknowledged it
and said sorry, between eleven and twelve I can't see
anybody, can't go to the hairdresser, I'll be playing Suppose. It's like Mah-Jongg—I guess, haven't played that
since I was twelve. Each player has a teak, or in the cheap
set cardboard, rack on the table in front of him and draws
from a pile, a sort of Pandora's box, of chips marked with
all sorts and degrees of disease and accident. Points are
given, not for cheering up, since that invites hypocrisy
and eludes scorekeeping, but just for appropriate suppos-
ings, and to quote the rulebook for all such games, the
player with the most points at the end wins. (Underpaid
writers take note: there's always a call for lucid, imaginative prose in commerce, excuse me, the private sector.)
One prohibition is supposing you're dead, or were never
born.

If you've lost a leg you can suppose it was both. If lungs
are the trouble, suppose it's your mind. If it's mind—but
then a friendly rival can drop you a hint, with gestures,
so you won't disgrace yourself; there are a few orange
chips that stand for becoming feeble-minded or just com-
mon-garden paranoiac and having arthritis, emphysema
and a choice of other difficulties besides. If you have plain
diabetes or hepatitis you obviously choose the newly developed varieties the medication for which has shrunk
you to a height of two feet. And so forth. If things really
couldn't be worse—but there are some conditions most
people don't like to play with, since you're not allowed

to bring in subsidiary factors such as love, religion or finances. This is a game for the more or less up-and-about, as a more sociable and less time-wasting form of what they're going to do anyway, that is, supposing how much worse it could be.

As I do. When not studying the contrary. Or more rarely, forgetting about it. Like settling into a new house, not nearly as pleasant as the one you loved so long and were forced to leave. Rotten luck, no point pretending otherwise, and the verb "settle" has unfortunate connotations—of unreliable landfill under the building, of accommodation to less, of the preposition "down" as applied to marriage and "up" for paying a bill. Nevertheless, in this new house it appears that one does eventually settle, up, down or sideways; just skip the pep talks and that false cheer we were going to examine and it might work out pretty well.

The cheer idea, by the way, didn't get dropped like a stitch but for cause. Too controversial; might get some people's backs up and we wouldn't want to do that, would we? Good spirits in adversity, chin up, keep smiling, that's one of our most sacred cows. I rather resented the slurs on it myself. False? neurotic? so you can't even feel good for a few minutes without berating yourself? There's our Scylla-and-Charybdis in a nutshell—Shrinksburg on one side, that's the whirlpool (some nut!) and Fat Sap grinning from the cliff on the other. I suggest a compromise. Keeping Affliction squarely in the foreground, let's say a few smiles a day won't be put down as too abnormally neurotic, just so the patient, I mean protagonist, sufferer, citizen, retains a good healthy capacity for gloom and despair at the same time, privately and nationally.

Snapshots just arrived, from one of our young companions there, of our wonderful hike through the gorge across Crete last June. Not all the way across; you corkscrew up in a bus first to the top of the divide. Eight hours we took on the walk, if walk you could call some of it. Prodge alone, or the Greek boy with us, would have done it in four or less, and we could have gone faster but there was no reason to, it was too amazing and beautiful to hurry through. Such towering oleanders I had never seen and for crags and boulders you could envy the Romantic poets their vocabulary. It's sometimes hard being deprived of words like "sublime." Homer with us all the way; hadn't gone far in the Iliad then but never felt him more a presence than that day, except more briefly at windy Mycenae, in front of the Lion Gate through which Agamemnon must have ridden out—in his chariot I suppose, or striding, I don't see him on horseback; the Trojans were the great horse-tamers—and ten years later rode or strode back to his immediate and horrid death. (Yes, Aeschylus has the palace in Argos a few miles away but I'd rather stick with Homer on that question, Mycenae being far more stimulating now.) No such man-made connection through the gorge, but stone and water, our feet and eyes no different from theirs on that trek, are connections enough. The grand split in the mountains must antedate Homer by a lot more than the time between him and us, though I put that as a question, my geology like too much else alas next to nil. But surely it did, and they knew the island well, through stories or their own excursions.

There was a contingent from Crete at Troy, and Odysseus in one of his wily fabrications, while still in disguise at home, calls himself a Cretan, younger brother of the leader Idomeneus. It was a real place to their eyes, not mythical; the image would be as clear to everyone as to us the skyline of Manhattan. It's their world we're knowing as we make it or rather it makes itself a part of ours. A permanent part. Eight hours that will have changed our lives as any true experience does, which is the only possible meaning of experience; aside from other charms of modest lodging and morning swim on that south shore, quite different from the north one in temperature, topography and what it draws the mind to. On that side you lean toward Africa, toward Egypt where Menelaus paused to get rich on *his* way home. Compelled, more than toward Europe because this has more of mystery, your thoughts skim and swerve and swoop for nourishment, high above remains of ships saved from burning at Troy and planes from World War II—to a fish's eye all equal palaces.

Spring rains had been heavy; river unusually high for early June, so after the long descent, not always close to the vertical but feeling like it most of the time, come places better negotiable by hoptoads. These are over wobbly stepping-stones evidently arranged for by the National Ministry of something or other, alongside the satin-smooth base of a rock wall rearing some hundreds of feet straight up from your shoulder, its opposite number—other side of the prehistoric cleft—just tantalizingly out of reach across the torrent. Similar stones mark some thirty or forty obligatory fords, where as in so much in life, passage on the side you're on becomes impossible. A

Greek woman in sandals and long black skirt and shawl, from the semi-deserted stone village toward the end, in her seventies at least and with a load of groceries, skips across the last of the fords, last before the sea, as though some goddess were giving her a quick lift and had every day of her life. Then she stops to look back, marveling at those of us who take a second or two to consider where the next foot should come down, or the awful prospect if it didn't. But the mile or two where the river goes underground and you walk along its dry rocky bed, although you miss the water, that's when Homer's voice seems most plain and present, from simple power of imagery perhaps, the delight of feeling the epics surging along beneath your very feet these three thousand years, to reappear at some moment in all their gallop and sparkle, fresh and truthful and mind-stretching as ever.

Stones, stones everywhere, many in arrested motion from some appalling slide not too remote in time, and the giant oleanders in bloom, pink, red and white, and olive groves and sheep and goats and stone enclosures for the small herds, and stone for every fence and wall of the dead village near the neck of the canyon and the partly living one farther on, where children play among ruins and an old man has placed his chair at the gate far from his house and with his back to it, for a look at passing hikers though July and August will be more rewarding that way. P. of course leaps over a bank and an assortment of boulders and is quickly gone from our sight, to discover exactly in what form and manner the river reemerges, and what kind of opening could accommodate such a mass of water. About the same, I imagine, as used to permit the Delphic or any other first-class oracle to give utterance. But that's just in reference to the size of the aperture. The actual spot at Delphi is more like the old stone well near our tennis court in Vermont, if that had a temple with priests instead of woods for its setting, and currently a bushel of tourists to every square inch of stone.

Hectic days, too much N.Y. for one week. But what a force of gravity the little island has, even now; how we would grieve and fume if we were barred from its bridges and tunnels. Of course it's too much for its mayors, poor things. It's too much for our thoughts too, of whatever brand. Personal memories, if nothing else, would undo us. My parents and grandparents weren't native New Yorkers, only lived there about two hundred and fifty years between them, never much at home. My godmother was, born and bred, it was her city, she was in exile all the years away from it as they were in it. The tugboat fleet is loaded to the gunnels with her dreams, and theirs, and Mr. Santini's.

Music mainly, and friends, keep us from gibbering on the sidewalk or slipping off one side or another, where the tide runs so fast. Lovely mystery—that such profusion of youthful gifts in performance, and the will to work that hard to develop them, keep coming along. Parlous times or not, there they are, another blessing to count. Ears relenting somewhat, simply couldn't go on being so peevish, just to spite another member of the team; one of these days might know why they make what they do of Mahler's ups and downs. A young duo, flute and viola, worth the voyage and more. Higher than moon-flights, heavenly

time-killer—ah, there it is, at last! The ski-lodge couple
were just our poor plodding parodies; it's what's made of
time that lets us out of it without loss of life. And sound,
where does that come in? Well at least there's none without duration; the rest you'll get in Aesthetics 105. Meanwhile the immediate givers of the strange geometry, the
players, ask for practically nothing in return, really only
the chance to stay alive and keep at it. Like the nightingale in the desolate garden in Geneva.

Then scramble for the 11:05 home and spooky walk
half a mile to where you had to leave the car earlier in the
day; ticket on wet windshield, hand of the law in the
night, nice feeling, they're on the job; as if there'd been
anywhere else to leave it. Terrific sense of pressure
around these suburban stations these days, empty out, fill
up, more and more, day after day, car doors slamming,
feet racing, hearts too, briefcases flying. Dawn there with
her coffee machine and early N.Y. Times, so much for her
fingertips of rose. But now it's still middle of the night and
you're briefly wondering, just in healthy sensible degree,
if the house has been broken into in your absence, while
the law was at work ticketing your car. Alarm System
Co. most prosperous business around, but I don't really
know that for a fact, maybe veterinary clinics doing as
well.

Our young poet friend David Y., still lacking ticket to
Mars and still scarred in the heart as now we see he always
will be by Mike's death, went to public reading with us,
out of reverence for the principal. He was right to revere
in that case, as we have for much longer and from much
closer, K. being eighty-six now and not prepared to say
die till it's done. Neither is the beautiful lady and painter
we are scarcely acquainted with, eighty-eight or nine,

there last night though not that time the chief lion. That
one, whose life-work was being celebrated a little more
than usual, is a kid in his upper seventies, our old friend
and several hundred other people's; has never taken the
trouble to have enemies, or worry about the flak from
some quarters. Toy-master to the world he is; and one of
equal wit if narrower frame, aged ninety-two (a different
evening), is the champion of an opposite kind of campaign
—civil rights; perhaps not so opposite really.

Of what used to be called heroic stature, these four
dashing ancients, two men, two women, who would blush
or be quite cross to hear it, having merely, along with
certain endowments by nature, prodigious habits of hard
work. Inflated reputations?—not these, but of course
sometimes. Any reputation is an inflation, just or prepos-
terous and for every decade some downright comical,
speaking only of the arts; business and politics get you
into quite another ("another ballgame" I will say only
under torture) ballgame. It's the way of the world, and
you can't be squawking at all its ways at once; have to
pick and choose.

But glory be, they still do get born, the truly great or
at least way out of the ordinary and not just at the bat or
in rock bands, and the strange thing is how in old age if
they reach it neither fame nor infirmities seem to have any
bearing on what they are or have done. Lucky the Greeks
were to so love the process of praising their own great.
No, not lucky, wise rather, as no other people have been.
Surely this must be a big part of the sheer pleasure of
reading Homer now. It is such relief, such a trip, it really
picks you up, to have all that admiration to breathe and

move around in. Because it's *good* admiration, given that Ares for all his rages wasn't quite the ultimate lunatic he has become for us. The standards were set and were very high, for spirit as much as physique. There were inferiors, second-class heroes or lower, but there is no false admiration, no honoring of the hustler, nothing for Balzac to make a story of. Or us. But we've about run through our stories for the time being. Maybe an infusion of honor, of no kind now generally recognized or remembered, would help.

But about those infirmities——

Ashamed, at no such venerable age whatever the repairman may think, to be dwelling on mine? I swore No shame! Must try to stick to that, and in fact don't feel overpoweringly unworthy, just not all that interested in the subject any more. Odd. Other people's far worse troubles didn't have that effect. What does is strong, work-obsessed, fun-loving, high-IQ types—preferably also gorgeous-looking at any age, scintillating, madly generous, athletic and not overly egomaniacal but you can't have everything—who barge along full steam to the end whenever that may be and don't quite give the thumb to adversity, which would be indelicate, but don't wear it on their sleeves; *and* whose work has changed the eye or heart or hope of the world. I mean for the better, not the way we're being taught to expect.

Tall order? Well, it's that or short shrift, no way between, so why not be Greek and look up for a change. Only our models—not speaking now of those other heroes of the ski-lift, tell you the truth I was partly fooling about them, something told me maybe they weren't all that great—I mean the really endowed and brave and

honest among us, will have to go it alone. No Olympus
to get a helping hand from, and probably no Moose in a
tent either when you come right down to it. We'll have
to settle for that.

So from some of that Homeric exposure and reflec-
tion, plus the excitement of leaf-life these past ten days or
so, something I meant to record has rather lost its juice.
Actually the leaves called for more attention—did they
always in October?—in case one should be seeing less of
them another year though it seems that's not inevitable.
Anyway, whether it is or not has become rather insignifi-
cant, I'll have to think why, certainly not from loving life
any less. Not just the mass of colors, of which my favorite
this year was the peculiar old-rose of some of the maples,
exactly the shade of Nora's big rug, hers and Yuri's. Just
as absorbing is the private, particular drama of each one,
in its turn from green to whichever of the reds and yel-
lows or combination thereof its death calls for, to the
incredible instant of the stem's giving way, and the last
proud pennant show in the flutter down, perhaps with
wind to skip it up and about a bit on the way, there to
start the definitive withering to brown that will crackle
under the rake and children jumping in the piles, as we
used to and P. and E. and their friends did too. Sad—the
only sad thing in all this; you don't see children doing that
any more, not here anyway. Burning's illegal, though car
fumes aren't, so the nice nutritious leaves go into hundreds of thousands of ugly green plastic bags, which
aren't illegal either, and the children are most likely at the
TV, since the disillusion with Little League.

Otherwise all very fine and invigorating; the best time. If we got individually down in the mouth over the death of the old year we'd have thrown in the sponge long before Homer. Not that we ought to take it lightly, of course; it must have been nice through all those millennia to have ritual ceremonies to sop up the mourning, and I love to think of the great bonfire high on the hill in Italy, in honor of All the Dead, to be seen far out at sea where Odysseus passed on his way to the interview with Tiresias and the shades of those he had been fond of. We acknowledge the deep import of the season too in our way, with plastic and even real pumpkins and festoons of toilet paper along the roads, though door to door trick-or-treating has fallen off sharply; too dangerous I suppose, except among friends or on campuses.

As I was saying, with the trees putting on their big show, and one of the most high-spirited and prolific of our elder artists too, it was impossible to hang on to, or recreate or sympathize with, the rage and grief of months ago, I think February or March. It was to go something like this.

But goddammit Doctor, can't you understand, I can't read! I can't read! Why should I want to live like that? Yes I know, it's not your business what I will or won't settle for, I'm only saying it because you're one of the few really good guys left in your profession. You're old-fashioned, you think people are people, you're wonderful. That shitty little technician down there at the hospital with those blazing lights in my eyes so I couldn't stand it and I blinked, I mean my eyelids did, there's such a thing as reflexes I suppose, and you know what he said? You won't believe it. He said, "Keep your eyes open, please." I said, "I can't." He said, "You're making a less than ade-

quate effort." I said, "Can't you talk English? Where did
you learn that TV-Watergate-Special hogwash verbiage
anyhow? The English for what you're trying to say is
'Try harder.' Even one of the biggies in the Private Sector
knows that much." I hope I said it. At the next machine
I started bawling buckets, film ruined I guess, couldn't
care less. That one, jerk number two, said, "We'll have the
pictures in about two weeks." I said, "Where do you come
from? Where were you brought up? I'm losing my vision
not by the day, by the hour, and you know damn well
there's no picture on earth it takes two weeks to develop.
We get them from Mars in ten minutes." That was a shot
in the dark; maybe it's two minutes.

We got them the next day and I might as well have
spared my breath, except for the public-service aspect.

Long ago—about seven months; the leaves we're scuf-
fling through hadn't begun to show their first pale baby-
green. Now their brown remains are thick on the lawn,
where we got rid of the latest upsurge of zoysia grass last
spring. Brown pine needles too. Some people don't realize
how much conifers shed, in a stiff wind. Must get out and
rake. Also feed or replace the pink hyacinths, and cut
back the rampant vines we find strangling half our trees
every fall—bittersweet, poison ivy, honeysuckle, mul-
tiflora roses and one I never can remember the name of,
with big, nearly round leaves and wicked thorns. That
and the poison ivy are indigenous with a vengeance but
some of the others, in our innocence years ago and needing ground-cover, we actually paid money for, via mail
order, they looked so good in the ads. Between them
they'd take over the state of Connecticut and Manhattan
too in no time if we weren't all keeping after them.

And then for heaven's sake, gods willing, by hook,

crook or Trojan horse, to work. KOFU's been fun, but as Homer so sublimely teaches, enough's enough. Solong, Moose, have a good day.